BROON FROM TROON

BROON FROM TROON

An autobiography

Gordon Brown

Stanley Paul
London Melbourne Sydney Auckland Johannesburg

Stanley Paul & Co. Ltd

An imprint of the Hutchinson Publishing Group

17–21 Conway Street, London W1P 6JD

Hutchinson Group (Australia) Pty Ltd
30–32 Cremorne Street, Richmond South, Victoria 3121
PO Box 151, Broadway, New South Wales 2007

Hutchinson Group (NZ) Ltd
32–34 View Road, PO Box 40-086, Glenfield, Auckland 10

Hutchinson Group (SA) Pty Ltd
PO Box 337, Bergvlei 2012, South Africa

First published 1983
© Gordon Brown 1983

Photo acknowledgements

For permission to reproduce copyright photographs in this book the
publishers would like to thank Colorsport, Ken Ferguson, G. G. R
Hofmeister, Kelman Photography, George McBride, Adrian Murrell,
Press Association, John Reason, Scotsman Publications Ltd and the
Scottish Daily Record

Photoset in Linotron Baskerville by
Rowland Phototypesetting Ltd, Bury St Edmunds, Suffolk

Printed in Great Britain by The Anchor Press Ltd
and bound by Wm Brendon & Son Ltd,
both of Tiptree, Essex

British Library Cataloguing in Publication Data
Brown, Gordon
    Broon from Troon.
    1. Brown, Gordon   2. Rugby football players –
    Scotland – Biography
    I. Title
    796.33′3′0924   GV944.9.B/

ISBN 0 09 150260 8

To Linda – the tiger in my tank! Thanks pal.
And to Mardi and Rory, without whose help this book
would have been finished in half the time

Contents

Foreword

by Bill Beaumont

British forwards proved themselves the best in the world in the seventies and consequently there could be no higher praise for Scotland and British Lions lock forward Gordon Brown than simply to say that he was the best middle-of-the-line player in Britain throughout that decade.

He was an outstanding jumper, a formidable scrummager and a surprisingly athletic and mobile player in the loose for such a giant of a man. As befits a low-handicap golfer, he was a natural ball player and had the temerity to score eight tries during the Lions tour of South Africa in 1974. He set a ridiculous standard for the rest of us donkeys to follow.

He was the cornerstone of the Scottish pack on thirty occasions and should have been so many more times. His talent was enormous and he played Test rugby on all three British Lions tours in the seventies.

I only played against him once at international level when England finished a distant second at Murrayfield in 1976. In that particular game, played in front of Her Majesty Queen Elizabeth and Prince Philip, Broonie was at his most majestic best. He produced a regal performance and he must have been an inspiration to his colleagues.

The following summer I was privileged to play alongside him shortly after I joined the British Lions in New Zealand as a replacement for the injured Nigel Horton. I quickly appreciated just what a great forward Gordon

9

was. A tough, ruthless competitor on the field of play, he was a great character off it.

Some players love touring on the other side of the world for three or four months and others hate it. Broon from Troon loved every single moment and his bubbling personality was invaluable on that ill-fated tour. I was resigned, albeit happily resigned, to playing in the 'dirt-trackers' team every Wednesday, leaving the stars to join battle in the big Saturday matches. As sixth choice for the Lions, I was just pleased to be in New Zealand at all.

In my first two matches against a Canterbury–Otago select and against West Coast Buller we rattled up 90 points in two thumping victories. The following Tuesday, four days before the second Test, I was surprised to find Gordon Brown joining me at lock forward for the game against the combined Marlborough–Nelson Bays team at Blenheim.

Then a couple of the senior players took me aside before the match and told me that if I had a really good match I would be in the Test side for Saturday. I couldn't believe it. It was a warm day at Blenheim and the game was played at a furious pace. We won 40–23, but with both sides running everything, I was absolutely whacked midway through the second half.

I had had a good game up to that point and loved playing with Gordon, but I turned to him at a scrum and said that I was on my knees, completely knackered and I couldn't keep the pace up any longer. He stared at me with those big, innocent, blue eyes and replied, 'We are going into that Test team together, come what may, and every time you slow down or opt out of anything in the last twenty minutes of this match, I'm going to belt you as hard as I can.' He drove me to the end of the game and the sequel worked out like a fairy tale. The Test team was read out the next morning and I was there alongside G. L. Brown.

For that I owe him a great debt. For everything he

accomplished in his nine years at the top, the game of rugby remains in his debt.

He was one of the last of a seemingly dying breed – a great player, a great character and a great tourist. He enjoyed a remarkable, yet controversial, career. He has a rare story to tell and, thanks to his honest forthright approach, a lot of light is thrown on Scottish and British rugby in the seventies to make this book such a thoroughly good read.

1

Hot Water

The 1976–77 season opened in a blaze of publicity. The new Scottish Rugby Union president, Hector Monro, MP for Dumfries and Galloway, was taking a very public stance against dirty play. He issued a warning to all that he and the committee would not tolerate this from anyone. If any international player transgressed, he would be unlikely to play for Scotland again. Many of the players in Scotland found it somewhat ironic that Hector Monro should take this stance now that he was president of the Scottish Rugby Union.

Had he not been president of the Langholm Rugby Club for the past twenty years, where one player in particular has continually dented this proud club's name with his history of violence on the field of play? As far as I know there has been no attempt by Hector Monro to have this player put out of the club – and rugby – once and for all.

There were some doubting Thomases amongst the rugby fraternity who questioned whether Hector Monro would stick to his guns. Their doubts were seemingly proved right when Jim Aitken, the Gala prop forward, who was not renowned for being a shrinking violet, was sent from the field one week and played the following Saturday. He received only a warning as to his future conduct.

I was selected to play for Glasgow against the North and Midlands in the Scottish Inter-District Championship. It was December 1976 and the game already had a jinx on it. It had been postponed from the week before when our team bus was unable to travel from Glasgow to Edinburgh because of snow. I had a dreadful time getting even to Glasgow that day, from Troon.

The referee was Jean-Pierre Bonnet from France. He was on an exchange mission. He should have refereed an earlier Glasgow versus Edinburgh match in the same championship, but it too had been postponed, due to frost.

As we travelled, successfully this time, on the bus to Edinburgh, Sandy Carmichael and I were running through the names of the opposition with some of our younger and less experienced team mates. When I came to the North and Midlands hooker, Allan Hardie, my comment was quite simply, 'He could be very much at home playing in Argentina!'

The game was not exactly stirring. We were making quite heavy weather of the task before us and they were working away not allowing the game to die on its feet. There was no atmosphere whatsoever as Murrayfield was fairly empty. There had been no aggression from anybody during the game, and Monsieur Bonnet was not being taxed in any way other than maybe in keeping his concentration.

Then midway through the second half my whole world collapsed about my ears. I drove into and through a loose ruck which had formed near to the touchline on the stand side. I had not obliterated anybody, stood on anybody, or killed the ball by my action. I was lying face down on top of one or two players when I felt someone grab my head with two hands. The hands momentarily held my head, then *wham!* A knee crashed into my face, bursting it open from my nose to my hairline. I howled out in agony. The pain racked my whole system and the blood spurted from the wound. My assailant still had hold of my head and I instantly thought, God, he's going to do it again. I struggled and twisted off the bodies and landed on the ground facing upwards with other bodies on top of me. I caught sight of my assailant's face for the first time – *Allan Hardie.*

14

'Hardie, you bastard!' I yelled as the blood pumped over my face.

'F— off, Brown!' he growled, and then he deliberately stamped on my face. The force actually lifted his other foot off the ground so that his whole weight was now being ground into my face. He then lost his balance and fell off my head. The agony of his studs grinding into the wound he had already inflicted I will never forget till my dying day. I yelled at him again and began pulling the bodies off to get at him!

At the back of my mind throughout this attack, which lasted fully twenty seconds, I was listening for the shrill blast of the referee's whistle. It never came. I pulled the last body off me and I was up and after him. Half blinded by my own blood and tasting it in my mouth, I caught him. I wanted to smash his teeth down his throat but instantly realized that my right hand would not achieve the desired effect. Instead, I hurled him to the ground and swung my right boot at him with every ounce of strength I could muster. I swung too early, damn it! It was my shin that caught him. He nevertheless lay as though he had been murdered. I obviously had not lost control completely otherwise he would have been seriously injured as he lay there.

At long, long last the referee's whistle sounded. He rushed over to me and as the blood flowed down my face, pointed me in the direction of the tunnel. Not just for the magic sponge treatment – I was off. I hesitated slightly to see what was to happen to my assailant and was relieved to see the referee point him to the tunnel, too. My blood rose to boiling point again, though, when Hardie turned to the main stand and had the audacity to appeal to the spectators with arms outstretched for help. I nearly hit him again. Ian McLauchlan, Glasgow's captain, grabbed me and told me to go straight to the dressing room as quickly as possible and not to speak to a single person. His voice brought me back to my senses.

John Frew, the Glasgow physio, arrived with a cool

sponge and towel and quietly led me away from the scene. As I turned into the tunnel, booing broke out from the few hundred spectators in the stand. I was heartbroken. I thought, Is it me they are booing? They've got it all wrong. Boo him. Boo Hardie. Not me. God, it *is* me! All they had seen was me chasing and booting Hardie. No wonder they were booing me. Had they not seen the blood on me? *Surely* they knew me better. I was heartbroken.

The bath in the dressing room was full to the brim with hot water, and at the time I didn't realize the hot water I'd got myself into! I was immediately admitted to the doctor's room under the stand. The doctor on duty was my old friend Donald McLeod. He had attended to my ailments many times over the years and had stitched me on a few occasions. Hadn't he had me back on the pitch at Dublin after stitching me up in two and a half minutes?

I lay down on his surgery table. He quickly examined me and said, 'My God. You're in some mess.'

I said to him, quite calmly, 'Thanks for these few words of comfort, Donald.'

He set about his task. 'You're badly torn internally, too,' he said. 'This'll probably leave quite a nasty scar.'

'You've set your standard in the past, Donald,' I said, 'don't let me down. I expect a perfect job.'

'Belt up before you make me nervous,' he quipped.

That little bit of patter between us helped immensely to cool me down. I was in the depths of despair and it was comforting to be in the company of Donald, a good friend.

'Were they booing me?' I asked him as he worked away at putting my face together again. He ignored me. 'The booing . . . as I left the pitch . . . was it at me?' I was almost scared to hear his reply.

He paused and then said quietly, 'No, I don't think so. Now shut up and let me concentrate on a real problem.'

For fully twenty minutes Donald McLeod gave me the benefit of all of his years of experience. Finally he was finished. 'Well, my boy, I've done a damned good job on that.' He meant it, and he had.

By then the game had finished and we had been joined by Ian McLauchlan. 'Jesus Christ, Broonie,' he said, 'that's not doing much for your good looks.' He was desperate to know what had happened on the field. He said that none of my team mates had seen anything of the incident because I had been on the far side of the ruck. Before I had a chance to answer, there was a quiet knock at the door. As Donald was still cleaning me up, Ian answered it. I could hear a quiet conversation at the door and Ian then came over to me and said, 'It's Allan Hardie at the door. He wants to come in and apologize to you. He says it was all an accident.'

My blood boiled instantly. 'If he comes in that bloody door I'll not be responsible for my actions,' I replied loudly. Hardie departed hastily.

Soon there was another knock at the door. It was one of the North and Midlands players. He entered gingerly, not knowing what sort of reception he was going to receive. He examined my face and quickly, with emotion, said to me, 'By playing alongside Allan Hardie, I have condoned his behaviour. I am ashamed. I am sorry.' With that, he left. I do not remember who he was, but I appreciate his coming to see me. Nobody else did.

I left Donald's wee room fully half an hour after I had entered it. I later learned from Donald that John Law, the secretary of the Scottish Rugby Union and a good friend, arrived to see how I was doing just after I had left.

I changed out of my blood-spattered gear, showered quickly and left Murrayfield stadium as soon as possible, accompanied by Bryan Gossman, my clubmate at West of Scotland who had played stand-off that day for Glasgow, and his wife Judi. I did not say much during the train journey from Edinburgh to Glasgow, being almost numbed by my experience, but I did appreciate Bryan and Judi's presence. On arriving at Glasgow I bought an evening sports paper and the full realization of exactly what had happened hit me. 'GORDON BROWN SENT OFF' was the headline. I was mortified. I hurried to find the train for Troon before anyone recognized me. I locked myself inside the toilet of the train for the journey, such was my embarrassment.

I had tried to telephone my wife Linda from Edinburgh to tell her the awful news personally, but without success. As I walked up the garden path to our home I thought, she'll die if she opens the door and sees me in this state. However, the television sports news had already broken the news to her. She knew that I must have been badly injured to react as I did. She was still horrified to see the extent of my injuries.

I watched the television replay of the incident that night and was very distressed at what I saw. The film proved one thing quite clearly – my injury was no accident.

For the next few days I was bombarded by the press. I was asked for quotes and reasons, but I said very little. I also refused to allow myself to be photographed because I did not think that would have been good for the image of rugby. I had tarnished it enough already. I looked like someone, or something, out of 'Dr Who'. My forehead, nose and eyes were badly swollen, my eyes almost closed. Both my eyes were blackened, and stitches running from between my eyes to my hairline looked like a zip. On the Sunday morning my daughter Mardi, then one and a half years old, had one look at me and ran out of the room in terror. After some time and reassurance from my wife, she slowly ventured back, first, peering round the door, then slowly and carefully coming closer. She eventually climbed onto my knees and snuggled into me. She remained there for the rest of the day.

I was overwhelmed by the enormous amount of sympathy which I received from both the public and the press. It all helped to ease the awful depression I had fallen into. I knew that what I had done on the field was wrong and I had deservedly been sent off. I knew that I would face my first ban ever by a disciplinary committee. It was impossible to reply to all of the many letters which I received. To each of the writers goes my heartfelt thanks.

I did, of course, receive some letters which were far from complimentary and I accepted them in the spirit in which they were written – with the good of the game of rugby at heart.

The waiting for the disciplinary meeting to be called seemed an eternity. I wanted to know immediately just how long I would be banned for. As a first-timer I reckoned I would receive four weeks, but the incident had been on television and therefore was notorious, so maybe that would add two more weeks. Six weeks – I had settled on that length of ban, ghastly though it was. It would mean my missing the England international at least. That did not particularly thrill me but I accepted that I would have to swallow my medicine.

The referee's report astounded me. He had written it immediately after the game without talking to anyone. In it he stated that he had seen me being kneed in the face and that I had chased Hardie to retaliate. Now all of that from start to finish took 45 seconds. Why did he not blow his whistle as soon as he saw me being attacked? Was he waiting for advantage? I think the referee fell down badly in his responsibilities. If he had blown immediately Hardie's knee had crashed into my face, I would not have suffered the stamping and I would not – and I repeat not – have retaliated as I did. I am not just passing the buck. Despite the fact that it was Hardie's knee that split my face open, it was his second assault which made me boil over and retaliate as I did.

Virtually everyone who witnessed the incident thought that my injury was caused by the stamping. Very few of them realized that a knee had been used initially – but the referee did!

I did not attend the disciplinary hearing. I pleaded guilty by letter and accepted that the referee's report was correct. What else could I do? I *was* guilty. I added to my letter a plea for leniency based on the fact that I had never been sent off before. I hoped the committee would take this into account when deciding my fate.

19

Fully one week after the committee meeting I had still not been told of the outcome. It was the week before Christmas and the mail was being delayed. I was going through mental hell. The press were constantly phoning me at my home and at my work and I thought that I would go round the bend with the pressure. Eventually the news broke – three months' ban. I wept. I knew I had been wrong, but three months! I could not believe it. I just could not believe it. A quick mental tally told me that I would miss all the internationals, and because of that, probably the Lions tour to New Zealand as well. I wept again and felt very bitter.

Hardie was banned for eighteen months. He should have been banned for life – *sine die*. No player who so coldly and calculatedly attempts to maim another is worth a second chance. *Ever!*

Again I was inundated by calls from the press, despite the fact that it was Christmas. I had to escape from the harassment. I loaded the car on Boxing Day and took my wife, daughter and myself off to my sister-in-law's in Aberdeen. When it was discovered where I had gone, word quickly spread round Troon that I had gone to find Allan Hardie, who lived in Aberdeen, to make the three months' ban worth while.

Before leaving for Aberdeen, I received a phone call from Dod Burrell, the tour manager for the forthcoming Lions tour to New Zealand. He was short and to the point. He advised me to keep in training during the term of my suspension because once it was over, if all that I required was match practice, then all might not be lost as far as my tour chances were concerned.

Despite Dod's phone call, which I sincerely appreciated, I could not find the motivation to don my tracksuit and get the bit between my teeth and start training. I felt very bitter towards rugby for the mental turmoil I was going through and yet at the same time I was discovering there was more to life than rugby football. All Saturday and Sunday to do as I pleased. No late-night training

sessions for West in Glasgow. So much more time to devote to my family and my business. One Saturday Linda
and I were invited to Ibrox stadium in Glasgow, as guests
of Rae Simpson, the Rangers FC chairman. After the
match, between Rangers and Partick Thistle, we were introduced to Jock Wallace, then the Rangers Manager. He
knew all about me and inquired about my fitness level,
although one look at me and he knew what it was – low.
He very generously invited me to train at Ibrox. 'I'll give
you a wee bit of help myself,' he remarked with a glint in
his eye. I thanked him and said I would contact him soon.

My meeting with Jock Wallace certainly stimulated
me, but I was still fighting my bitter mental battle and at
times felt so low about rugby that I almost decided never
to play again at any level. Even the carrot of a Lions tour
could not lift me; in fact it magnified my mental turmoil. I
had to clear my mind and start to get all the bitterness out
of my system. If I were to have the option of going on the
Lions tour I had to start training. I phoned Jock Wallace.

I could have trained at West of Scotland, but I had no
desire to listen to the banter of the players about their
matches and any incidents and not be part of it. It would
have been rubbing salt into the wound. The same went for
watching them play on Saturdays. I just could not do it.
This did not endear me to some of the West members.
They thought that I should have devoted myself to the
club during my time out of the game, especially since the
club had appealed to the Scottish Rugby Union to recon-
sider the length of my ban. This was a move which I
sincerely appreciated even though it was a forlorn one.

My training stints at Ibrox, under Jock Wallace, initially, then Tom Craig, the team physio, were hard, very
hard. Jock trained with me most of the time, doing all the
work he was asking me to do except lapping the track and
sprint shuttle runs. His driving voice never let up. He
coaxed, cajoled and clouted me, and after two weeks he
said, 'Right, sonny, that's the rough edges knocked off.
Now we can get into some serious training.'

21

I revelled in the banter of the Rangers players. I could enjoy it to the full without it bugging me as it would have done at West. They were talking about games and incidents that I was never part of. I loved it when Jock let me train with the players and take part in actual football games. I did not do too badly either! Of course, the players took the mickey out of me but that made me feel part of it all.

Mark you, I got my own back on them one day when I took in a few rugby balls and Jock insisted on using them in training. John Greig would have made a great rugby player.

One day Jock was giving me a real workout. The climax had me sprinting up the steep terracing – all the way to the top. I was to do it ten times, but after seven I was shattered and said that I could not do any more. He quietly said, 'Is that so – we'll see.' After one minute's rest he took my pulse and after a few seconds he ordered me to the top again. I managed it, but only just.

This time he gave me two minutes' rest and after taking my pulse, sent me off again. I managed eventually to reach the top. I was all in. I could scarcely breathe. I was dizzy. My body was racked with pain. Jock's booming voice brought tears to my eyes. 'Only one to go.' I did not think I would be able to go *down* the terracing never mind come back up it again.

After two minutes I set off again. It was agony. He was barking at my heels. I had to make it to the top. My lungs, legs, arms and head were bursting. I made it. I hung over a crush barrier and vomited. My stomach retched five or six times. I thought I was going to die. I just wanted to be left alone, hanging there, to die in peace. Jock came across to me and said, 'Bloody guid, son. Now come away inside before you catch a chill.' I was dumbfounded. One minute he was trying to murder me, the next he was concerned about my catching a chill. Quite a man is Jock Wallace.

Despite all the training and fun I was experiencing at Ibrox, I was still unsure about my future in rugby. 'Do I want to go away and leave my wife and daughter for four months, after all we've been through?' That question kept ringing round and round my head. The resentment I felt towards rugby was still burning in my mind.

Slowly, as the countdown started to my return, I began to feel more and more like playing again. I was welcomed back to West with open arms and that made me feel good. I had often wondered what sort of reception I would receive after staying away so long. I started training at West and was gently honed back into rugby fitness. My general fitness was magnificent, thanks to Jock Wallace and Tom Craig, but there is no substitute for a real scrummage or a few mauls.

The press were full of stories of my making a comeback to the Scotland team to play Wales in the last game of the Five Nations Championship. I was named as a member of the international squad after playing in only one club game for West against Glasgow University. I then had one more game against Edinburgh Wanderers for West on the Saturday before the Welsh game. The international team was to be announced the following day. The Wanderers game was very poor and patchy and I felt that I had never got going at all. Nevertheless, the selectors knew what I could produce when asked. The ball was firmly in their court.

At the squad session on the Sunday I waited with all the other players for the chairman of the selectors, Tom Pearson, to announce the team. The papers were all in favour of picking me and the general chat amongst the players was that I would be in. I refused to be built up too much, though, and had decided that what was to be would be. Of course I wanted to be picked.

Tom Pearson entered the room and after exchanging pleasantries with some people, he came across to me. He took me to one side and asked, 'How are you feeling after your car accident on Thursday night?' He was referring to a three-car pile-up in which I had been involved on my way home to Troon after training at West. My car was a complete write-off but, thanks to my wearing a seatbelt, I was uninjured apart from some bruising.

'I'm feeling great, thanks, Tom,' I replied, enthusiastically.

'Good, as long as there are no after effects,' he replied, and off he went.

'Ya beauty!' I yelled, inwardly and silently. 'I'm in the team.' Why else would he inquire about my health at such a time?

Tom read out the team to the squad – no G. L. Brown! I was dumbfounded. I was angry at myself for letting my guard down. One minute, cloud nine, the next, the deepest dungeons of the earth. I showed no emotion but inside I was terribly disappointed. If Tom Pearson had not spoken to me before announcing the team, I would have been all right. Disappointed naturally. But I would have accepted my non-selection as a failure to impress in terms of match fitness or even as a move to protect me. I could have slept more easily at night with such thoughts in mind.

I was used as cannon fodder by the Scottish pack for the whole of the squad session. I did not enjoy it. I returned home to Troon that night a very humble person.

On the morning of the international I played in Edinburgh for West against Stewarts/Melville. To say that I had a certain feeling of anticlimax playing in that game is an understatement. I did not stay in Edinburgh for the international, having decided instead to watch it at home on television with friends. Unfortunately, my car broke down on the way and I was left stranded at High Blantyre, a small village in the middle of Lanarkshire. Hunting feverishly for a television to watch the game, I eventually found a small hotel and politely explained my predicament to the manageress. She apologized, saying that the only television was in the residents' lounge which was packed. Just then a voice boomed out, 'Gordon Brown, bach, what are you doing here?' My eyes focused on a Welsh supporter bedecked in red and white scarf, rosette

24

and tammy. Instantly I was whisked into the lounge to be greeted with an incredible sight. Dozens of Welshmen! All of them up for the game but not one of them with a ticket. I was given a rapturous welcome by them all and a seat right in front of the television.

They had all been across to Edinburgh that morning to visit Murrayfield and walk the length of Princes Street – 'just to take in the atmosphere of the city'. The atmosphere they created inside that wee lounge in High Blantyre made me feel as if I were at Murrayfield. The fact that they did not actually attend the match was of no significance to them. 'It's the trip we all love most', I was advised. 'The match itself isn't so important. Mind you, we don't tell that to the wives.'

We all settled down for the match with every limb in the room as comfortably accommodated as possible and with every pair of eyes fixed to the small screen. Imagine my astonishment when, on the first few chords of 'Land of my Fathers' by the Murrayfield band, each and every one of them stood to attention to sing with pride and passion. I marvelled at their patriotism and it brought a lump to my throat. How I wish the Scots were able to do likewise.

My disappointment at being excluded from the Welsh game was softened by my appointment as branch manager of the new Glasgow office of the Bristol and West Building Society. It gave me plenty to think about. The Bristol and West had only recently spread its branch network into Scotland so I had a marvellous challenge on my hands to stimulate new business. But despite the motivation my new post gave me, I was still dogged by mental anguish about my future in rugby. I wanted to keep playing and I wanted to go to New Zealand, but I still could not allay the bitterness burning inside me.

My controversial situation certainly engendered interest in me in the business community in Glasgow and therefore was stimulating the society's name. The Bristol and West management were very keen that I should go to New Zealand for this very reason.

25

I was delighted to receive, through Mike Gibson, an invitation to go to Bermuda to play in the annual Bermuda Irish versus Rest of Bermuda challenge match. I flew out from Heathrow on the day the names of the Lions tour party were to be disclosed. My flight was at noon and the team was being announced at 1 p.m. Luckily I had just sold my house in Troon to Bill Aitchison, the senior air-traffic controller at Prestwick airport, from where all North Atlantic flights are monitored. He agreed to listen to the team announcement and radio the plane with the news.

Imagine my feelings when at around 1.10 p.m. aboard the plane the steward came up the aisle calling out my name. I quickly identified myself and he thrust a large gin and tonic into my hand and barked, 'Captain's compliments, sir. You're a British Lion!' I downed the drink in one.

My hosts in Bermuda were John and Denise Kane. John was president of the Bermuda Rugby Union and he quickly informed me that in honour of my selection for the Lions tour of New Zealand I would be captain of the Bermuda Irish team.

The island holds this rugby festival every year, and over a four-day period, the social calendar is extremely hectic. Cocktail parties abound and the whole atmosphere is extremely friendly and pleasant. Add to this bright blue skies, pink coral beaches and warm light blue sea and you have a good picture of Bermuda and the contented rugby fraternity. It was during this trip that I witnessed for the first time females playing rugby – serious rugby! There were two teams from Boston representing Boston Ladies Rugby Club and Beantown Ladies Rugby Club, and could they play! Full-blooded tackling, rucking and scrummaging were all there to be seen – even the odd punch-up. It was really peculiar to be standing in the bar of the rugby club with a group of females discussing the different techniques of scrummaging and line-out blocking.

I led Bermuda Irish to victory and was proud to receive the Challenge Cup at the end of what was a hard, though enjoyable, match. The referee admittedly had helped us unwittingly a few times, but then, isn't that the luck of the Irish?

In the Lions party there were quite a few surprise names and they were mostly Welsh. Three Scots, in particular, were unlucky to be omitted, Ian McLauchlan, Sandy Carmichael and Jim Renwick. Ian McLauchlan's omission was rather political, I fear. His impressive record plus his commanding personality off the field were probably seen as a threat to the overall control and influence of Phil Bennett and John Dawes.

During the weekend get-together in London I was terribly uneasy. I was still not sure if I should be there at all and I spent many hours walking the streets of Richmond with my mind in torment. Outwardly I was showing no stress whatsoever, which was probably a mistake, but my misgivings I had to work out for myself.

The ironic part of the weekend was on the Saturday night when, under the guise of choirmaster, I had to lead the boys in a singsong. The management team decided that we should all have an after-dinner singsong in the team room. Many of the boys wanted to disappear instead for a few hours to the bright lights of London and took quite badly to the restriction placed on them. They were reluctant singers and that night I was a reluctant choirmaster!

When we flew out of Heathrow I was embarking on the longest flight of my life. Throughout the journey to New Zealand – and that is a long, long journey – I could not accept that I was finally in as deep, with rugby, as I had ever been before my sending-off. On arriving in New Zealand I thought, Brown, you are here so make the most of it. I then vowed that no matter how the tour finished, I would return home a success. I was not going to go through all that mental trauma for nothing!

2

On Top Down Under

I had been to New Zealand before, in 1971, when I was a proud member of the Lions team which toured New Zealand and Australia. It will probably go down in history as the finest Lions tour of all time. We defeated the All Blacks and wrested the world crown from them for the first time since they themselves regained it from South Africa.

It was one of the great experiences of my rugby career. My wife Linda said, 'You went to New Zealand a boy and came back a man.' During the tour, I reached a level of commitment and determination that was way beyond my wildest dreams. The tour was my introduction to the super-star world of rugby. I liked it. I discovered that I was able to produce my best form under the most severe pressure. I was also able to bury the tag of 'Big Softy' for ever. This was a tag that had been hung on me ever since I started playing rugby. A Lions tour is the pinnacle of any British rugby player's career. To travel, eat, sleep, train and most of all play alongside the greatest rugby players in Britain, was magnificent. Players I had played against and had admired for years even from my junior days at Marr College.

I had to become a better player through touring with them. There would be so much to learn from them, just by watching them and listening to them. With ten caps already won, my rugby career was well and truly launched, but I felt that this tour was going to make it really take off. I dedicated myself to learning and to improving my game during the tour. I knew that I would have no finer opportunity. It was a perfect challenge to me. I revelled in the company of all of the big stars like Barry John, Mike Gibson, Gareth Edwards, Willie John McBride and Delme Thomas. They all had my full respect and I was determined to gain theirs on and off the field. I was incredibly nervous at the start, I felt so young and inexperienced despite the caps I had won and despite the tours I had made to Australia and Argentina with Scotland in the two previous years.

We had a mock game of rugby league in London when the team assembled and I remember shouting to Gerald Davies during this game for a pass. I got it! I felt so chuffed that Gerald had not ignored me, that he had actually been happy enough to give me the ball. A simple thing like that worked wonders for my confidence in such company. The spontaneous outburst of singing instigated by the Welsh members of the team on our bus trip from London to Eastbourne further helped me because I was able to join in and feel I was one of them. The humour of Bob Hiller and 'Chico' Hopkins allowed me to laugh with everyone too. It was so important to me to be one of the team off the field because I knew I would take that feeling with me on to the field.

My selection for the tour came at the end of a very hard season which had included Scotland's defeat by 19 points to 18 at Murrayfield by Wales and Scotland's magnificent victory by 16 points to 15 over England at Twickenham – our first victory there since 1938. It was during this game that I had a running physical battle with Nigel Horton, the bruising England second-row forward, and the way I handled myself seemed to convince some of the selectors that I was not the rookie they had thought.

Two days after our victory at Twickenham the Lions team was announced and it was my brother Peter, who had kicked the winning conversion against England on the Saturday, who telephoned me at my office. He shouted down the phone 'How does it feel to be a Lion?' You can

29

imagine what my reaction was. A loud 'Yahoo' rent the air. Peter had been unavailable for selection for the tour and although he was obviously disappointed, his feelings were somewhat softened by my selection. He was absolutely delighted for me. One of my first phone calls thereafter was to my fiancée Linda Hastings to tell her of my selection and to discuss a new date for our wedding, which had been fixed for July, right in the middle of the tour.

The Lions team gathered in London, and after we had been kitted out, we went down to Eastbourne and I will always remember that bus journey for the way the boys sang. It was completely off the cuff, nobody orchestrated it, it just seemed to happen. It was something that became a major feature of the tour. We even sang in the mornings as we went from the hotel to the training ground. We didn't just sing rugby songs either; we sang pop songs, and ballads, with a few golden oldies from some of the more mature members of the team.

The week at Eastbourne was sheer purgatory. Carwyn James, our coach, put us through our paces often twice a day, and despite wanting to work 100 per cent and impress, I, along with twenty-nine other players, always had the fear of being injured and therefore not being able to board the plane at the end of the week to fly to Australia and New Zealand and finally become a true British Lion. We all knew only too well that training at Eastbourne doesn't make anybody a Lion.

Carwyn's appointment was a magnificent decision by the Four Home Unions tours committee. He was an out-and-out coach, the first time such an appointment had been made for a Lions tour. I took to him and to his authority immediately I met him. I knew that I would work for him during the tour. This commitment allied to my appetite for rugby made an excellent recipe for success.

There were some bizarre happenings during that week in Eastbourne. The line-out practices were like all-in wrestling matches. Carwyn insisted that we practise our line-outs in such a manner because, as he put it, 'This is how you're going to do it in New Zealand because that's how they do it, so you might as well get used to it.' Little did I realize just how right he was. He was a fervent Welsh nationalist and took great delight in teaching us to sing 'Sospanfach' in Welsh during that first week. He went out of his way to make sure that John Spencer, England's skipper, was word and pronunciation perfect. Spencer rose to Carwyn's challenge magnificently.

One night we were given a rousing and confident talk by Ray Williams, the Welsh coaching adviser, who had recently been in New Zealand watching them play. He was confident that if we played to our capabilities we could win but he did say it would take one hell of an effort. We certainly had the ability. Virtually all the internationals who had played during the season were available for selection. It was almost as if there was a feeling among the players that this tour was going to be something special and we wanted to be part of that.

Ray McLoughlin, the Irish prop forward, took over the running of the forwards during the week at Eastbourne. It was his job to organize us for scrummaging and give us strengthening exercises. I'll never forget the first session he took when he barked, 'Thirty press-ups. Begin.' I managed only three and stopped. He was dumbfounded. 'You surely can do more than three press-ups?'

'No,' I replied. 'Three is my maximum.' He looked to the heavens and exclaimed something like, 'God, here we are going to New Zealand, Colin Meads and all, with boys in our second row.' By the end of the week, I could do three sets of thirty press-ups. Ray McLoughlin had a certain way of getting things done and I had a determination second to none. I felt a great sense of relief when I finally got on the aircraft at London airport. That week at Eastbourne was the longest week of my whole life.

When we arrived in Australia I was selected to play for the first game in Queensland and although I felt fit and

31

eager to do well in my first game as a Lion I was bitterly disappointed at the outcome. It turned out that we were all suffering from circadian-disrhythmia (Dr Doug Smith's medical mumbo-jumbo for jet lag) which meant that our bodies had not adjusted to the time change. Midway through the second half I felt so terrible I just wanted to lie down and die. We lost the game and I felt very low afterwards. Doug Smith, the team manager, did his very best along with Carwyn to cheer us all up, but no matter how they tried – and I appreciated their efforts – I was miserable.

My mood was not improved either by the attitude of the Australian players. The Queenslanders made no allowances for our jet lag. They murdered us as best they could. One of the Queensland players, a prop called Dave Dunworth of the Brothers Club, revelled in our circumstances. At a reception laid on for us after the game he gave me a verbal lashing. 'Last year we kicked shit out of Scotland and you guys did nothing about it. We did the same again today and again you guys just laid down without a fight.' His white teeth shone through his big grin and it summed up his sneering contempt for our non-physical way of playing the game and especially for our apparent lack of retaliation. I wish we had played against him on our way home. Many of the refereeing decisions were unbelievable too. We were all relieved when we narrowly beat Sydney three days later and finally left for New Zealand.

We received a magnificent welcome at Auckland airport on our arrival. Everyone was delighted to see us. We were welcomed like lambs to the slaughter. We had a week to settle in before the first game and I must admit that this was just a wee bit too long. We were all itching to get at the New Zealanders and finally get the tour under way. It was almost as if we were ignoring the two games that we had played in Australia. It was as if they had just never happened and did not count. Carwyn trained us hard during the first week and in particular we practised our line-outs *à la* New Zealand. At first the New Zealand newspapermen thought that we were taking the mickey. Then they realized that we were deadly serious. I gave Carwyn ten out of ten again because the line-outs we practised were exactly like the way we had to play for the whole tour. I developed an all-in wrestling technique along with my supposed prowess as a jumper. The combination of the two was to help me and see me through the tour successfully. Never has the saying 'when in Rome' been more aptly applied.

The variety of training sessions which Carwyn gave us during the week was fabulous. It set the standard for his training sessions for the whole tour. The sessions were never boring nor irrelevant. They were always concise and constructive and demanded the highest commitment, effort and concentration. Thankfully, I was selected for the first game in New Zealand; I was burning to play.

In the stadium before the kick-off I was as nervous as I have ever been in my whole rugby career. The game went like a bomb for me and for the whole team. We completely crushed the opposition forwards. The expected robust play from the New Zealand forwards simply did not materialize. In fact the only two people who were penalized by the referee for over-robust play during the game were my team mate, Derek Quinnell, and myself. I had been quickly nicknamed 'Baby-Face Broon' by the press, and after this game one of the banner headlines in the sports pages stated: 'THIS BABY-FACE BROON IS A REAL MEANY'. I had a bit of a chuckle over that one.

For the next few days I marvelled at the fact that I was now a true British Lion player. I had barely been away from Troon for two weeks, but it seemed like two months. I felt I could now relax and settle in to the tour. Having finally played and been victorious, I now felt that a colossal burden had been taken from my shoulders.

Our team had a marvellous make-up, and I realize now that the tour had all the ingredients for success. We had a big, strong pack; we could scrummage because we had the world's greatest technicians in that department. We had magnificent backs; a first-class coach; an excellent manager; very, very good weather; plenty of leisure activities each day to take us away from the hotel and away from the training paddock. We were a team that had a great spirit and pride in itself; a team capable of making many friends among the public. In general we had excellent rapport with the press. But most of all, we had individuals who were rugby players of the highest calibre, who could produce their tremendous ability at the right time within the framework of the team.

Our backs were superb. Their play rewarded us in the forwards for our efforts and encouraged us to even greater efforts to earn more and more ball for them. We jumped higher, ran faster, scrummaged harder as the tour progressed. These backs, of course, were stars, but the youngsters in the team, like myself, were determined to show these heavenly rugby bodies that there was a bit more to this team than them. So we had a brilliant establishment and an enthusiastic younger generation. And we had Carwyn James to weld us into a winning machine.

I did not play in either of the next two matches. This disturbed me somewhat because I did not understand nor appreciate (because nobody told me) that this was part and parcel of touring – that it was not and could not be taken for granted that one would play in alternate games. I responded to this seeming omission by training even harder in the hope that this would encourage my selection for the next game which was against the New Zealand Maoris. I was selected.

Many people anticipated a fast free-flowing match full of all the things that are good in rugby. Alas, it was not to be. The game was full of open thuggery. The Maori players came onto the field, in front of 48,000 people, like demented animals. Their eyes were nearly popping out of their heads such was their overmotivated state. The game was vicious, dirty and crude. Many incidents happened in full view of the referee, David Millar of Otago, especially one punch from Baker which split Sean Lynch's bottom lip so badly he needed fourteen stitches. Yet Millar did nothing but dish out penalty after penalty – no warnings, not even to Baker! It was a fight for survival and we soon learned to check the rearview mirror at all times!

Unfortunately, it seemed that an article on the possible phasing-out of Maori rugby had incensed and aroused all the wrong passions in these proud people. Even John Spencer was seen to retaliate late in the game after being on the receiving end from Ken Going. As we left the pitch to go back into the dressing room at full time I'll never forget Willie John McBride's laconic words: 'Welcome to New Zealand, son. This is what it's all about.'

This type of rugby certainly did not appeal to me one little bit but it did teach me how to defend myself and how to get on with the job in hand. The lessons I learned in that game were to stay with me not only for that tour but for all the other tours I was to undertake, especially as a British Lion. To survive, you simply had to be prepared to defend yourself.

Socially, the tour had started extremely well for the team. Every afternoon, we were given ample opportunity to take up invitations to golf, sightsee, hunt deer, go jet-boating, or whatever. There were also many invitations from the public to go to their homes for dinner. This was always welcomed as it came as a pleasant break from the hotel routine. Initially, I suspect that the pleasant, happy relationship we had with the press and public was largely because they never thought for one minute that we were actually going to beat the All Blacks. This led to a Jekyll-and-Hyde attitude towards us. Away from the rugby ground, no one could do enough for us or be nicer to us, but at the grounds and during the matches, the crowds were generally hostile towards us, despite the magnificent rugby we played. I was aware of the crowd's demand for victory from their home teams, and if this victory was not forthcoming, they seemed to demand our blood as an alternative. One crowd which could not call for anything other than maybe sympathy was at Wellington. They had to stand by and watch their team, their proud team, being annihilated. We scored 47 points that afternoon. It was a proud day to be British.

Everything we had worked for came to fruition. All the pieces of the jigsaw fell into place. For weeks Carwyn had been telling the New Zealand press that we were still only in third gear. 'One day we will click into top gear,' he said. 'Then you will see something.' They would have loved to have scoffed at him, but as we had been winning all our matches, they dared not. If ever a man's words came true, they did at Wellington.

The whole team was superb, but I will always remember the match as the one when Mike Gibson played probably the finest game of his life, and that is saying something, because I believe that Mike is the greatest rugby player the world has seen. He has the ability to be brilliant at just about everything in this game of ours. Throughout my tours around the world his has been the one name which is always talked about when the discussions get round to top players. Mike's greatest asset was his instinctive running off the ball. His pure footballing brain shone through as he ghosted into attacking support positions. His ability to read a situation was unequalled, and he had all the skills.

The many reports of different peaks in 'Gibbo's' playing career only serve to illustrate the length of time this man has been playing with an exceptionally high level of consistency. For me his peak was in New Zealand in 1971. He displayed all the attacking and defensive qualities I had only dreamed of seeing in one player. Gibbo could turn it on wherever he was playing and he certainly did that day at Athletic Park, Wellington.

I sometimes wonder if what the Lions did to Wellington explains why Canterbury played such an appalling game of calculated thuggery against us a fortnight later. Canterbury had had a week to digest the implications of the biggest affront to New Zealand's rugby side in living memory, and they had another week to work out what to do about it. The sums they did, and the conclusions they reached, were a disgrace both to the game and to their country.

In that game Sandy Carmichael was the victim of an assault in comparison with which my own troubles with Allan Hardie pale into insignificance. In the first scrum, Sandy was punched in the face by Alister Hopkinson, his opponent, and afterwards was struck so often and so hard that he sustained a multiple fracture of the cheekbone and had to come off. Derek Quinnell and I were on the substitutes' bench and were so incensed at what was happening to our team mates on the field that we were practically fighting each other as to who would be his replacement. Sandy went back on the pitch, however, only to have his face smashed even more. He sustained the grand total of five fractures of the cheekbone on a day when the sun shone overhead and all he wanted to do was play rugby for Britain – fairly and squarely.

But there was nothing on the level in that match. The Canterbury forwards were frighteningly overmotivated and seemed prepared to stoop to the lowest level of gutter thuggery to satisfy their lust for blood. With Hopkinson, Wyllie and Penrose in the driving seat, they kicked, punched and elbowed anyone in a red jersey who came anywhere near the ball. It was a wonder that nobody was killed. The obscene utterances of the spectators, who were baying for more and more Lions' blood, reminded me of films I had seen of Romans screaming obsessively at gladiatorial combats.

In the hotel that night I sat down opposite Sandy at dinner. One look at his puffed, purple, black and blue face, his closed left eye and almost closed right eye, made me sick to the pit of my stomach. I was deeply saddened that the tour was going to lose one of the finest and fairest players in the game of rugby. The culprit could maybe lick him at throwing punches but he could not match his skill. The sight of Sandy's face put me right off my dinner but it

37

did foster in me a resolution for the rest of that tour and any other tour I might go on – I would survive.

One of the most amazing features of the match had been the referee's statement to both skippers during the second half that he was going to follow the ball and totally ignore what was going on elsewhere. This, to me, was as irresponsible as anything else that happened that day. It must have been sweet music to the ears of certain Canterbury forwards. It was as though the sheriff of Dodge City had intimated to all the murderous gunslingers in the town that he would officiate only over clean-draw challenges in the middle of the street but he was not interested in what skulduggery might happen in the saloons, whorehouses, and back alleys.

Our dressing room after the match was like a battle-ground. Few players did not immediately require medical treatment and the whole place had an air of doom and gloom about it, despite the fact that we had actually won the match. That atmosphere changed dramatically that very evening when an amazing feeling of togetherness, an all-for-one and one-for-all attitude, oozed through the whole party. That welded us in a manner that not even the talented gifts of Carwyn James could possibly have achieved. That battle against Canterbury taught us that we, as Lions, had to get our retaliation in first. If there was going to be any blood spilled during the remainder of the tour we were going to make sure it was New Zealand blood and not British. The singing which had started on that bus journey between London and Eastbourne continued. No matter where we went on a journey we automatically, spontaneously started singing. It was the one time when we were able to give vent to the great feeling which existed between us all. The longer the tour progressed the more the touring party broke up into who was singing bass and who was singing the melody and who was singing descant. J. P. R. Williams and John Spencer were a magnificent duo on descant. The touring party was also being continually entertained by the superb humour of Bob Hiller, the Harlequins fullback, and Chico Hopkins, the Maesteg scrum half.

Our victory in the first test match at Dunedin was a victory for skill, guts, determination and bravery. It set the whole tour alight and meant that the tour was now alive until the final Test. Just before the full-time whistle the word was passed along the Lions bench where I was sitting that we were to accept both the final whistle and victory with quiet and dignity. Consequently when the referee blew for full time, we calmly stood up, shook hands with each other, shook hands with the All Blacks reserves and walked downstairs under the tunnel to the dressing room. Once inside we jumped six feet in the air and yahood as we had never done before. There followed fully twenty minutes of uncontrolled cuddling, back slapping and whoopeeing, the like of which I had never seen in my life before.

We celebrated our victory at Queenstown, a holiday spa right in the middle of the southern Alps. It was a very happy time and at last the gloom of Canterbury was put behind us. One of the relaxations on offer was deerstalking. Willie John had been looking forward to this for weeks because he had been here on a previous Lions tour in 1966. On that occasion he had been out of luck, but this time he had the top tracker-guide at his disposal and he promised him a stag 'as long as he did not mind a bit of climbing'. Willie John was so elated at our Test victory that he would have climbed Everest without thinking about it.

Half a dozen of us set off at dawn on a journey to the foothills of the nearby mountains where we were each allocated a guide who was to lead us on a hunt for stag. One of the guides' most important tasks was to make sure that we all kept a safe distance from each other. Imagine if Willie John had survived Canterbury and won the first Test only to be shot by a team mate!

My guide was George McBride, a farmer from Southland and a cousin of Willie John's. We set off to explore our allocated zone with George leading at a steady pace and me carrying the .22 rifle complete with telescopic sights. The rain fell steadily all day and after shooting at and missing, much to George's amusement, half a dozen stags, all of which George had stalked perfectly, we decided to head back to base camp, which was a farmhouse in the valley at the foot of the mountain. By this time I was absolutely shattered. We had been on the go for about eight hours and at times had been crawling through undergrowth and negotiating steep climbs, with only short breaks in between for some chocolate, our sole source of nourishment.

We were only about a mile from base camp when we saw a stag in the middle of a field away to our right. It seemed somewhat ironic that we had spent the whole day in the rain up the mountain and now here was a beauty almost on the farm doorstep. It took us half an hour to circle round the stag to get downwind of it. The last fifty yards we had to negotiate on our hands and knees. Finally at a range of about eighty yards I settled down lying full length on my stomach and focused him in my sights. Slowly I squeezed the trigger with George whispering last-second coaching lessons into my ear at the same time. Bang went the gun. The stag leaped into the air and bolted away. My disbelief at missing was quickly dispelled by George saying, 'You've got him. You've got him.' At that the beast keeled over dead, after travelling barely twenty yards. I was absolutely elated. I jumped to my feet and punched the air in a victory salute, screaming, 'Yahoo! You beauty!' At that instant, a voice from a hundred yards to my right boomed out, 'Brown, you bastard!' It was Willie John. He had been up to the top of the highest mountain, down it and round it umpteen times and had never seen a single stag, let alone shoot away and miss as I had done. He was back at the farm when he spotted the stag from the window. Redonning his wet gear, he circled in the opposite direction from George and me to get downwind and he actually had the beast in his gunsights when I fired.

Fortunately the harmony of the tour was not affected! Despite the fact that there was an obvious first team and an obvious second team within the touring party, we were never separated as individuals, not even by my pinching Willie's stag. We continued to roll through the tour as one party. The general underlying feeling among the players was togetherness. The Canterbury match had a lot to do with this. As Barry John said afterwards, 'I got bruises just by watching.'

Carwyn must have sensed what sort of a game the match against Canterbury would be, which was why he kept Barry out of it. Barry certainly repaid the debt in the first Test, and for the rest of the tour. He had a nickname in New Zealand which put him in his proper place and left him and everyone else in no doubt of his status. It was 'King'. He was a majestic player, and what a character as well. He was rarely less than brilliant, whether playing for club, country or charity. He scored more memorable individual tries than anyone I have ever seen, yet had the capacity to be a great team man too. I could write a chapter on its own about the King, such are the vivid memories I have of him both on and off the field.

The calm which he displayed before and during the tensest matches amazed and helped me. At team talks he generally sat in a corner with his eyes closed in apparent meditation, almost as if he was saying to himself, 'The team talk is for the lads – now what am I going to do today?' During the whole of the tour I cannot recall skipper John Dawes once referring to Barry at team talks. Barry would have done his own thing anyway.

He dominated the first Test in New Zealand with kicking that was pure perfection. Time and again he forced back the All Blacks' tidal wave and won for his team mates some welcome respite. Fergie McCormick, the New Zealand fullback, was tortured by Barry that day. In fact, he was made to look so bad that he was dropped afterwards, never to play for his country again.

Barry made everything look so simple and effortless,

41

whether it was kicking a massive goal, dummying, side-stepping or sprinting. All the photographs I have seen of him running with the ball look as if he is just cantering along, wondering what to do next. It is only when I look at the pained faces of the players trying to catch up with him that I realize the speed with which he must have been covering the ground.

My favourite try of Barry's was against New Zealand Universities. From a scrum to the right of the Universities' posts he dummied to drop a goal, broke open to the left, dummied one man and then produced a series of immaculate – ah, the master at work – side-steps to waltz past a dozen defenders and score between the posts. Pure class. And all of it done in dead silence.

At the beginning of that game, he uncharacteristically dropped the first three passes Chico Hopkins threw out to him. As the third one hit the deck, he burst out laughing. That night I was sharing a room with him and I asked him why. His reply was pure B.J.

'Have you ever seen me drop a ball before?'

'No,' I replied.

'Well, to see me drop three in succession must have had you worried?'

'Yes,' I said.

'How did you feel after you had seen me laughing?'

When I replied, 'Fine,' he said, 'That's why I burst out laughing. I didn't want you donks to be concerned – 'cause I wasn't.' Perhaps I should explain that he called all forwards donkeys.

I once asked Barry just how much he owed to Gareth's long spin pass. He talked glowingly about the extra time it gave him to react to situations, and so on, and he finished by saying, 'Mind you, Gareth's pass is now so long and so accurate I just stamp it "approved" on its way past!' Barry John was, for me, the original super-star of rugby.

One of the greatest strengths of that 1971 Lions team was that it was full of such beautiful playing contrasts. Barry John was all instinct, subtlety and confidence. Mike

Gibson was as clinical as a top surgeon. Gerald Davies ran as if he could win the Olympic 100 metres. John Bevan ran as if he could go straight through a brick wall. David Duckham ran as if he could go up it or round it. Gareth Edwards ran as if he could do all three. John Dawes played as if he were conducting the Berlin Philharmonic. And J. P. R. Williams played as if he were the Berlin Wall itself.

I am convinced that J.P.R. is the greatest fullback the world of rugby will ever see. He was magnificent. He had it all. His defence was as solid as a rock. His attacking sorties were like a volcano erupting. His fielding of a high ball, no matter how much pressure was on him, was perfect and unflinching. He was not a great kicker, but very rarely missed touch. He was an inspiration.

He had many brilliant moments in his long, illustrious career for Wales and for the Lions, but the one which to me demonstrated perfectly this man's natural ability was in the second Test in New Zealand in 1971. He was covering back into the Lions 25 to his fullback position in a very dazed state after being pummelled by the All Blacks pack near halfway, when he was called upon to field an enormous up-and-under kick from Sid Going, the New Zealand scrum half. He not only caught it, but immediately burst away to the open side, outflanking the charging All Blacks. He ran powerfully to the halfway line before giving a lovely pass to Mike Gibson. Mike drew the covering defence and released Gerald Davies to sprint to the goal line after beautifully avoiding a desperate covering tackle from McNaughton. As Gerald plonked the ball down at the posts J.P.R., who had supported him all the way, collapsed in a heap. But he recovered sufficiently to continue.

His determination and concentration in defence were exemplified by his tackle, which saved the match, on Sid Going against North Auckland. The famous Going brothers' scissors move was enacted to the full, yet J.P.R. refused to be drawn by the many scissors and dummy scissors in front of him. Instead he waited until someone finally burst with the ball. Sid did, going like a bomb. J.P.R. exploded him!

David Duckham was a revelation in that game against North Auckland, too. Of all the purple passages he treated us to on that tour, his classic was against North Auckland when, with no room to spare, he produced an unbeliev-able swerve-cum-side-step to score in the corner.

Strangely enough, I had first come across David four years earlier, before anyone had ever heard of him. I was playing in the Barclays Bank Inter-District sevens tourna-ment at Ealing. The biggest stumbling block for us (the British Linen Bank) was in the semi-final against Bir-mingham District. They had a player who, throughout the tournament, seemed to score every time he got the ball. He was big, fast and strong. He had an enormous side-step and a colossal dummy. I remember thinking, 'Mister, you'll go far!' He did.

In New Zealand, he really put it together, and although he missed the first Test because of John Bevan's amazing burst of form, he played in the rest with power, grace and penetration. In the final Test, his defensive qualities were put on trial and he came through with flying colours.

In the second Test he would have caught Ian Kirk-patrick – when Kirkpatrick scored his wonderful try after breaking from a maul at halfway and running past and beyond everyone – had he not been so blatantly ob-structed by Hunter, the All Blacks right winger.

The 1971 Lions certainly had a wonderful array of talent in the backs. I remember Mick Williment, who had played fullback for New Zealand, turning on the New Zealanders who rubbished Wellington for the way the Lions slaughtered them. Williment was a Wellingtonian himself, and he said, 'Barry John is the best first five I've ever seen; Mike Gibson is the best centre I've ever seen; J. P. R. Williams is the best fullback I've ever seen; and Gerald Davies is the best wing I've ever seen. Where is the disgrace in losing to a team like that?'

Will there ever be another Gerald Davies? I doubt it. I join with Mick Williment. Gerald must be the most thrilling wing I have seen. His side-step at full speed was devastating. Amid the carnage of our game against Hawke's Bay, Gerald scored four tries – all gems! The fact that they were greeted in total silence by the Napier crowd typified their attitude to us, and their ignorance.

That game against Hawke's Bay was another watershed in the Lions' development, although perhaps bloodshed would be a better way to describe it. Our new attitude to physical intimidation after the Canterbury holocaust earned us much instant respect from players and teams thereafter. But deep down we suspected that there would be a similar contest waiting for us farther along the line. It came against Hawke's Bay.

The Bay props, Thimbleby and Meech, both seemed out to challenge Canterbury's Hopkinson for the 'King Thug Prop' crown, such was their indulgence in all that is bad for rugby, and for the recipients' health. The Napier crowd was of the same gutter standard as the Christchurch crowd, which made it easier, somehow, to understand the gladiator feeling that both Canterbury and Hawke's Bay players experienced. They obviously felt pressurized into living up to the disgraceful demands from the terraces.

By the end of the match, such was the feeling on and off the pitch that I ran for the dressing room on hearing the referee's final whistle. Again, as happened at too many after-match functions, we stayed on our side of the room and the Bay players stayed on theirs. Hands across the sea cannot count for much when, for the previous hour and a half, those hands have been bunched into fists.

My own career as a British Lions Test match player began in the third Test in New Zealand, with the series square at one all. The build-up to this Test began during our short holiday break in Waitangi, in the Bay of Islands. As we arrived, the room pairings were read out. I was in

45

with Willie John McBride. Normally the two locks playing in the next game share a room and so I was excited by
the implications. The management pointed out that as the
Test team had not yet been finalized, nothing was to be
read into these room pairings. That did not stop me
licking my lips because there was no way that Willie John
and his great friend Delme Thomas would have been split
up otherwise. Willie John had a say in the selection of the
Test team, but he gave nothing away.

Finally, the team was announced and I was confirmed
as his partner to lock the scrum for Britain. I told Willie
John I was delighted. I wasn't exactly looking for him to
say, 'Well done, you've deserved it. You've been playing
really well,' but I had hoped that he might open up and
offer me some hint of encouragement or congratulations.
His reply dumbfounded me. 'I know who I wanted for this
team,' was all he said. I did not know whether he wanted
me, or whether he had voted for Delme to be retained and
was outvoted, or what. I suspect he wanted Delme. If his
reply was designed to act as a spur to me, to prove that my
selection was justified, then he succeeded. I'll make sure
you hang your hat on my peg for ever, was the silent vow I
made, and I trained during the build-up with a zest I had
never known before.

On the day of the Test at Wellington, I brushed my
teeth just before we left the hotel to make our way to the
ground. I can remember looking at my teeth in the
bathroom mirror and thinking, I wonder if they'll all still
be there tonight? I wore no mouth guard in those days.

The scene at the ground was good. The wind was
negligible (my prayers were answered), the pitch was firm
and the sun was shining. The dressing room was basic and
stark. I set about my preparation for the game. Suddenly
Barry John let out a great yell of disgust. 'I've left my boots
in the hotel.' We all immediately felt some degree of panic
because it had taken us half an hour to travel to the ground
and, with the increased traffic as the kick-off grew nearer,
there was no way the boots could be picked up and

brought back before the kick-off in forty-five minutes' time.

Barry as usual showed less emotion. He calmly sought out a police motorcyclist and sent him off to the hotel at top speed to pick up his boots. As the kick-off drew nearer and nearer, John Dawes was building his team talk to a climax and yet virtually the only thing on all our minds was 'When will that bloomin' policeman appear with Barry's boots?' Barry was the kingpin of the tour and it was unthinkable that he should play in someone else's boots.

With only a few minutes remaining and with Barry apparently asleep in a quiet corner of the dressing room, the door burst open and in came the policeman frantically and triumphantly waving the boots. 'I've got them, Mr John.' Barry immediately took them, thanked him sincerely, and laughingly said, 'You haven't brushed them!'

The game could not have started better for me and the rest of the team. We seemed to be clicking in all phases of the game and gained almost a monopoly of possession. My line-out pressures were eased dramatically by the withdrawal from the All Blacks team of Peter Whiting. I was able to dominate his replacement, Brian Lochore, the former All Blacks captain. We raced to an amazing lead of 13–0 in no time, and our scores, two goals and a drop goal, all resulted from quality play and individual brilliance.

John Taylor, the bearded Welshman, magnificently tackled Bruce Hunter, the flying All Blacks winger, inside their 25 and a ruck quickly formed. Willie John and I creamed the ruck and the ball was laid back to Gareth like a wee egg. Gareth's quick pass to Barry did the rest, enabling Barry coolly to drop the goal. Gareth's brilliance set up the next try. He burst at speed around the remains of an untidy line-out and handed off Burgess, the All Blacks stand-off, with such force that his body was lifted off the ground. As he drew the fullback, Barry materialized at his shoulder to take his silky pass and ghost over at the posts. Then Gerald Davies squeezed over the line to

47

score his try by manufacturing space out of nothing next to the corner flag. Barry converted from the touchline.

The All Blacks came much more into the game in the second half but we managed to limit them to one try only. The All Blacks centre, Joseph, might have scored later on in the game if he had not fallen over a dog which had strayed onto the field.

Our jubilation at the final whistle was immense because, being two games to one up, we all knew that we could not now lose the series. I had not lost any teeth either! What a party we had that weekend.

When we had calmed down and had time to think, we all realized how much we owed to Carwyn James. I know that a coach can only deal with the material at his disposal, that there is no sense in trying for hours to coach a player in something which is technically beyond him, but the best coaches astutely weigh up the existing skills of each player in their charge and work at enhancing those skills and blending them into a framework which produces a team playing to the maximum of its capability. Never should a team be asked to produce the impossible.

Once a high level of individual and team skill is produced, the coach's job thereafter is to ensure that it is sustained. Regular practice of basic skills is the means to this, as long as the content of the practice is of good quality. Backs must concentrate on alignment and passing the ball quickly and accurately. For forwards, scrums and line-outs must have priority.

Coaches must be psychologists too! Assessment of the temperament of players is paramount if the coach is going to extract full benefit from a practice or a game. The dividing line between giving a team a hard-slog session and a light fun session can sometimes be very fine, yet the consequences may be very different. In New Zealand in 1971 Carwyn James was a master at reading the signs and feeling the temperature of a situation. After the second Test, which we lost, he murdered us on the Monday morning. It was pure punishment, but not, as many suspected, for losing the Test but for the overindulgence practised over the weekend. Losing that Test, making the series one all, somehow seemed to take the pressure off us and we had made the most of it on the Saturday night and all day Sunday. Carwyn soon had us back to reality! We trained non-stop for two-and-a-half hours in the mud and rain and when he finally blew his whistle to finish, I did not have the energy left to walk the short distance to the dressing room. I crawled. I was still in my sodden gear when Carwyn came in and announced that the fifteen who were selected to play in the Wednesday match against Wairarapa-Bush were to report for training that afternoon at 2.30 p.m.

I went straight to bed as soon as we returned to the hotel and stayed there until 2.25 p.m. To my surprise, though, once we had warmed up in the afternoon and eased the stiffness from the morning's efforts, I felt great. It was a marvellous boost to know that I was so fit. I also gave Carwyn ten out of ten for his psychology, because the following day he took us to the beach and golf course instead of training. This had us raring to go for the game on Wednesday.

On the Monday following the Hawke's Bay game, we were all feeling one degree under as the team bus drove us to the training ground. Our hangovers were nothing to do with our weekend revelry, which had been silly rather than excessive. They were a direct reaction to the awful game against Hawke's Bay, to the brutality of the exchanges, the hostility of the crowd, and the hellish atmosphere at the after-match function. As the bus drew up at the dressing-room door and the usual posse of pressmen and public flocked forward, Carwyn stood up and shouted to the baggage man, George Earney, 'Put these rugby balls away – we're playing soccer today!' We were dumbfounded. We could not believe our ears. 'Mike, Gareth, John, Willie John, Swerve and Bas, pick four men each for a five-a-side competition.'

49

We were cock-a-hoop. The blues were blown away in one stroke. We had a great session, with Gareth, Barry, Mike and Chris Rea displaying their soccer talents to the full. The New Zealand press thought that Carwyn had cracked up. By the end of the morning, the tour was back on the road.

This tour party was blessed with magnificent running backs, all of whom could take on, and beat, an opposing player with natural flair and skill. It was, therefore, imperative that they be utilized fully by being given every opportunity to run with the ball. Our brilliant wingers in particular had to be brought into play whenever possible. Appreciating this, but not wishing to rely totally on the forwards for the possession necessary to launch these wizards, Carwyn came up with a simple but amazingly effective tactic. Any one of us fielding a kick from the opposition inside our half had to sprint towards the nearest touchline and scissor with the winger. This move shifted the target, the fielder, as quickly as possible and launched a runner into the open side of play where he'd find plenty of support from his expectant team mates. With virtually all our backs being gifted runners off the ball, they would be there.

Carwyn came up trumps too with the tremendous variety of his sessions. We had to work hard – we expected to – but we were never bored as he made the sessions as interesting as possible.

He was a great man for 'clinics'. If he felt that any player could benefit from an individual session then he 'invited' that player back to the training ground in the afternoon. It could be for fitness or skill training and it always seemed to have the desired effect on those who participated. Early in the tour, Chico Hopkins, our cheeky, chunky scrum half, required his reactions and handling to be sharper – despite his general excellent level of fitness. Carwyn saw to it.

He suitably punished the shirkers or messers at training. 'One lap' would be his command and we would all look to see at whom the finger was pointing. The culprit would then have to run the perimeter of the pitch while we all received a welcome rest.

All this produced a great feeling of confidence in the team, a confidence that grew with our achievements on the field.

We were incredibly lucky with the weather too. It was one of the sunniest winters for years, and the photograph of Barry John shielding his eyes from the sun during the match at Invercargill, of all places, somehow epitomized the feeling of warmth and wellbeing among us. The excellent weather meant that we could practise and play the way we wanted, and even when the weather turned sour, as it did in Greymouth, David Duckham scored six tries.

I came to realize later, when that element was missing, how important confidence is to back play. Even the greatest backs, such as we had in 1971, have to have their confidence built by constant practice and by mastering the basic skills of passing. Carwyn used to say, 'I don't care about moves. You can use as many as you like. You can do a quadruple scissors if you want to – just as long as you can pass the ball quickly enough and accurately enough under pressure to perform those moves without making a mistake.' From the first week of the tour, the backs had to practise those basics, and the longer the tour went on, the faster the ball moved until in the end it fairly whizzed from one side of the pitch to the other. It rocketed from one player to the next and was rarely mis-handled. Forwards hate to see hard-won ball wasted, and those 1971 Lions backs were a joy for us donkeys to behold.

It was the tour, too, in which British forward play came of age in the physical sense. Thanks to decades of superior diet and open-air life, New Zealanders and South Africans had always grown bigger than 'the Pommies' and so were able to dominate us physically. By 1971, though, the difference in physique was fast disappearing. We were nearly as big as they were, and all we had to do then was

51

come to terms with the brutality which was a part of their game. This was largely a matter of discovering the scale of the problem and then having the resolve to deal with it. We did both. Many fine men who teach rugby in Britain and Ireland were appalled at what we had to do, and so, I think, were most of us, but at least for the first time in living memory, we had the guns and the tanks with which to fight.

Any doubts that I might have had on the subject were swiftly dispelled in the final Test at Auckland. In only the second line-out Peter Whiting punched me in the eye, splitting the skin open like a melon being knifed. 'Jazz' Muller, the gargantuan prop, first grabbed hold of me by the throat as soon as the ball was thrown into the line-out by the All Blacks, then a moment later – wham! The attack must have been premeditated, otherwise Muller would not have turned round to grab me, standing at five, from his position at four, when the ball was thrown to Meads, in front of him at three. I had to go off the field to have the wound bound and protected. The cut later required six stitches. While I was off, New Zealand scored a try from a set scrum deep inside our 25, making the most of their numerical superiority. We fought back from being down 8–0 to 8–8 just before half time. There were some heated moments as the tension increased, with Muller being the sinner more often than not.

With fifteen minutes of the match left, my tour came to an abrupt end. Jazz Muller, who had mumbled some sort of warning to me moments earlier in a ruck, kicked a great gaping chunk out of my right leg just below the knee. What a bastard! When I saw the size of the hole I feared the worst, and when John Dawes had a look at it he confirmed my fears, saying, 'My God, you must go off immediately!' As I limped to the touchline I wept with anguish and despair. But I was soon cheered by the sight of Delme Thomas, a colossus of a man, appearing at the tunnel to replace me. He looked in such great physical condition, his biceps positively bulging, and was so

52

obviously straining at the leash to get onto the park, that even the crowd was awed.

The thought ran through my head, 'How on earth did I manage to keep him out of the team?' Big Del, a lovely man, yelled at me just before he took the field, 'Don't worry, Broonie, we're not going to lose this one now.' And nor did we, either. The match ended as a 14–14 draw and the series was ours. I was rushed to the hospital to have fourteen stitches inserted in my leg wound, which made twenty in all, including my eye. As far as my leg was concerned, it was really a matter of tucking in the edges. There was no way the wound could be closed over, it was so wide.

In view of what Peter Whiting did to me in that final Test, and the way in which the deed was obviously planned and organized, it may come as a surprise that I unhesitatingly rate him the top second-row forward I have played against, either for Marr, West of Scotland, the Barbarians, Scotland or the Lions. His line-out play was the most skilled and competitive I have ever encountered. He had the edge on me in height, but I'm sure he was always aware of my presence. The incident in the Test may have had more behind it than the fact that I represented a competitive challenge. He had been taking some stick from some New Zealand players and journalists who thought he could not look after himself in the hurly-burly of big-time rugby. I did not try to retaliate on returning to the fray. I was too busy trying to win the damned ball off him. That was far more important.

Some years later my phone rang at home and a voice shouted out to me, 'This is Peter Whiting, the bugger that split your eye open in New Zealand. I'm touring Scotland and I'll be at your home in six hours' time. Get the beer on ice and the beds made up!' He arrived and made himself completely at home. He was very welcome. I cooked some big steaks and the beer took a belting. That, to me, was what rugby stood for.

When I returned to New Zealand in 1977 with the

53

Lions, Peter was not available for selection for the games against us. I was relieved and disappointed. We did, however, have one further meeting in a restaurant. He bought me a steak to return the hospitality he had received at Troon. This was certainly one time he completely overshadowed me – the steak was four times the size of the one I had cooked for him!

I realize now that we should have rubbed the All Blacks' noses in the dirt in the last quarter of an hour of that final Test, when we had them on the ropes, instead of playing for a draw. But that draw gave us the series. What is more, it gave us the series by exactly the margin our cheerful and capable manager, Dr Doug Smith, said we would win by before we even played a game. He promptly became christened the Sage of Orsett.

I made many friends in New Zealand, though sadly not too many on the field. Peter Whiting was one of the few. The after-match functions, which were always attended by both teams, did very little to improve the atmosphere. There was always a them-and-us feeling. I never enjoyed this aspect of the tour. For me rugby has always been a game for extending friendships after the full-time whistle. The home teams were obviously disappointed when they lost, a natural reaction as they had been building up to a match with the Lions over a period of at least six months. We could have mixed with them much more than we did. We could have gone out of our way more than we did. It was probably one of the few black marks against the team during the whole tour. We were extremely open towards the public away from the rugby ground, whether we were visiting schools, hospitals, or rotary clubs. We were always good at extending and receiving the hand of friendship. I remember visiting a hospital with Barry John and Mike Roberts. Barry said to one of the patients, who was lying in bed, 'I'm Barry John, halfback,' and Mike Roberts then said, 'I'm Mike Roberts, bad back.' I hasten to add Mike was suffering at the time from a sore back.

Sadly, the good will shown to us off the field was not re-peated when we were actually playing. I was fed up with the attitude of New Zealand crowds. They never seemed to applaud our magnificent back play. Some of our glorious tries were scored in total silence. The crowds seemed to love it when any of us was injured.

During the tour, I learned a completely new attitude towards rugby. It was a cold, clinical attitude. This was especially so at the Test matches which were different from international matches I had played at home in the Five Nations Championship. They were more like a job in hand rather than the gala-day atmosphere of an inter-national at home. My level of concentration hit a new peak. I was tuned in for every second for every minute of the game. I suppose that was what turned me into a man. We were the enemy within and therefore we had to keep driving ourselves all the time. The extra lifts I got during the game came from the efforts of my team mates and the cajoling and inspiration of Willie John McBride. I learned a lot from Willie during the tour, especially in respect of scrummaging and attitude towards the opposition. He was unbowed, unbending and he set an example for me to follow. I got the distinct impression from Willie that he thought of me as the young pretender.

The tour made me a much stronger person physically. It made me have a much harder mental attitude towards the game, certainly so far as winning was concerned. I learned to value fully the relationship I had with my team mates and how important it was to have a successful relationship off the field as well as on it. The success of the 1971 Lions in New Zealand literally changed my life. Back home in Scotland I was treated like a hero. Suddenly I was a far greater celebrity than I had ever been before when I had *only* played for Scotland. Everyone wanted to hear my story about the Lions tour. I was inundated with invitations to speak at dinners. Surely there had never before been such a response to any tour abroad. Nor was that all. The success of the tour certainly proved an excellent launching pad for my new career in the world of business. I had just left banking to work in the building society, and suddenly, everyone was coming to me to invest their money.

3

Down Under Down Under

The Lions tour of New Zealand in 1977 was a different story. Mike Gibson, Derek Quinnell and I were the only three Lions to survive from the 1971 tour, and so we were in a position to make comparisons. It was inevitable that we should do so, each in our different ways and from our different standpoints, just as it was inevitable that the rugby communities and the media of New Zealand and of Britain and Ireland should make the same comparisons. The pity was that the Lions management of 1977, 'Dod' Burrell and John Dawes, did not accept that those comparisons were inevitable and treat them philosophically. They would have spared themselves a lot of misery if they had done so.

The first week of the 1977 tour was very peculiar. The lack of super-stars within the tour party meant a lack of definition. I certainly felt that we should all have to work hard to develop a team character, because there was a dangerous sameness about us all. Every team needs its stars for the majority to look up to, for them to respect, and to attempt to emulate.

I had an awful rash which ran in a broad band almost encircling my waist. It was sore and uncomfortable, especially during training, but I tried to ignore it. After a week or so I had the remains of the rash examined by a doctor. He told me I had had shingles – no wonder it was sore.

Mike Gibson ricked his back during the first week's training and he never fully recovered during the rest of the tour. He had, by his standards, a disappointing tour, but his advice should have been sought instead of ignored in our search throughout the tour for a blending back division. It never ceased to amaze me that the two men who had helped mastermind the brilliance of the 1971 Lions backs, Mike Gibson and John Dawes, could not get together to eradicate our problems outside the scrum.

This tour threw me in alongside one of my greatest adversaries, Nigel Horton. Six years earlier, we had been involved in a memorable battle when Scotland played England at Twickenham, and in the course of the contest I had become convinced that Horton's mission in life was to finish any of the odds and ends of business which the English armies had left unfinished at Flodden and Culloden. It was a bit like playing against a Centurion tank with mine-sweeping flails attached, and even when I went to shake his hand afterwards, he knocked my hand aside. Yet here we were, chosen to play for the same Lions team. During our first day in London, I strode up to him, hand outstretched, and said, 'Hi, Nigel. Congratulations on your selection.' He did not knock my hand away this time. The hatchet was buried. He was a fully committed competitor at all times, whether training or playing. I and many of my team mates received many bumps from him as he crashed about at training, and he did sometimes go over the score at line-out practices. He was never one for the pranks of touring, either. He never carried on or let his hair down, that I can remember. Even the simple downing in one of a beer if late for a team meeting received the cold shoulder from him, much to the displeasure of the rest of the team.

We had only been in New Zealand a few days when the fine weather broke and remained comprehensively shattered till the last few weeks of the tour. It rained and rained and rained. Sometimes it was damned cold into the bargain.

My first game of the tour was against Hawke's Bay, at Napier, scene of the filthy encounter on the 1971 tour. I

was desperate to get one real game under my belt at last,
having been out of rugby for most of the season. I had
missed the big time. Our coach, John Dawes, gave us a
long, hard scrummaging session the day before the match.
I doubted his wisdom at the time and the lacklustre way
we performed during the game confirmed that it had been
a big mistake. Obviously, we were not as fit as our coach
thought.

Despite being desperate for action, I found it hard to
react to certain situations which developed in the game.
As a result of my long lay-off, I was all at sea in the
line-out, in particular – physically and mentally. The
Hawke's Bay skipper, Robbie Stuart, had a field day
against me. Testing my patience well beyond the normal
limit, he bumped me, impeded me and pushed me. It was
almost as if he had known that because of my troubled
season he could commit mayhem and I would never react.
He was right. His harrying was probably the best thing
that could have happened to me so early in the trip
because it meant that I had to sort myself out mentally
well before the tour reached a serious stage.

I hardly won a ball during the whole game. On their
throw to the front of the line-out, if I stood at one, they
lobbed over me to two. If I stood at two, they bulleted
it to number one. I tried to organize Allan Martin, my
second-row partner, to cover the lob to two from his
position at four, or Fran Cotton to cover the low, hard ball
to one from his position at one, but neither scheme worked
out. The outcome was that I had the mickey taken out of
me completely. I was really humbled. Robbie Stuart
could not believe his luck. He could knock me about at will
on my throws and he could win the ball on his own. He
must still smile at the thought of it.

I vowed after that match that I would not be pushed
about like that again, despite the disquieting thoughts of
being sent off which flashed through my mind. It was a
constructive decision, because word of Robbie Stuart's
success spread like wildfire round the rugby-mad country.

Every second-row forward began licking his lips at the thought of doing the same to G. L. Brown. I was to disappoint them all.

I had had a bad cold before the Hawke's Bay game and had hoped that I might sweat it out during the match. Some hope. It was even worse afterwards. It stuck with me through the following week, which included the Taranaki match, until I was finally laid low at Taumaranui when it developed into flu. I was in bed for four days and felt low and lonely. My room mate Mike Gibson quite rightly immediately moved out to safeguard himself from infection, and despite many of the boys popping in for a few seconds, I felt completely out of things. I even missed our magnificent victory at Taumaranui over King Country-Wanganui, including Andy Irvine's five tries. One person who called to see me and who actually sat down for half an hour and braved the germs was the coach to the King Country-Wanganui team – Colin Meads. He had heard that I had been laid low and made the effort to come and see me. His visit cheered me up and was sincerely appreciated. One man of whom I saw little because of my illness was a local school teacher, Jack Morrison. He was the man who started me playing rugby at Troon Primary School, seventeen years earlier.

The flu took its toll. I missed the next two extremely hard matches against Manawatu and Otago, both of which we struggled to win. At last, though, I was fit enough to be considered for the Southland game at Invercargill, which was only my third appearance in eight matches. Not quite what was required of a player who had already missed most of the season at home. At the same stage of the 1974 Lions tour to South Africa I had played in six of the first eight matches and had scored two tries.

My main job against Southland was to deny Frank Oliver, their probable Test lock, any good possession at the front of the line-outs. I succeeded. At the same time, Allan Martin, my partner, had all of our ball thrown to him in the middle of the line-outs. My role was somewhat frustrating, albeit, to those in the know, successful.

The next game against the New Zealand Universities team was my last opportunity to stake a belated claim for a place in the team for the Test four days later. I had rid myself of flu and its aftermath and I was raring to go. Unfortunately, the majority of my team mates resembled walking wounded. Everyone who, through recent injury or illness, had little chance of making the Test team seemed to be playing. We did not play well. Many of my team mates were tentative and the Universities players revelled in it. In the end, despite having enough chances, we were soundly beaten by 21 points to 9. It was the first defeat of a Lions team by a provincial side since 1968.

I did not finish the game. I suffered a partially sprung cromium clavicular joint in my right shoulder. It was caused by a Universities forward crashing into me with his knees as I moved in to support Moss Keane, who had just fielded a kick-off. The pain was excruciating and I thought that my shoulder was smashed. The culprit was none other than Garry Brown, the Universities lock and a protégé of Jack Morrison, at Taumaranui. I remained on the field for ten minutes or so in the hope that the pain would subside, but it increased. I had no option but to call it a day.

As I walked slowly and sadly to the dressing room, the thought ran through my mind that for me this tour was just never meant to be. I had hardly entered the dressing room when Moss Keane joined me, having been kicked in the head by an opposing player.

The following morning, we all gathered in the team room to listen to the Test team announcement. I was amazed when John Dawes told us that we had all been considered fit and available for selection. I immediately dismissed this announcement as John's way of trying to boost the confidence of those selected. I soon discovered that he told the press the same story. I did not like that at all. There was no way that I was fit to play in the Test and I was certainly not the only one – not by a long shot.

After we had been told the Test team, John Dawes advised us that we were going to have a very exacting training session that morning. We were told that if we did not want to join in we had only to say so, but if we did start the session, then we had to finish it. 'Remember,' he warned, 'it will be hard.' However, it was not a choice we were being offered, but rather an ultimatum. 'Come out and train and suffer with your team mates or go home today,' seemed to me to be a more realistic interpretation.

As I walked to the training field from the hotel, I was jostled by quite a few pressmen. They all wanted to know if I agreed with John Dawes that I was available for selection for the Test. I loyally replied that I was available. Inside I was hurt. I was being used.

The training session was physically the worst and mentally the most horrendous I had ever been involved in. It seemed to last for hours and I was only partly involved. The pain in my shoulder was crippling and my right arm was totally useless. I scrummaged only as a wing forward, using my left shoulder as the point of contact.

The whole touring party looked upon this session as a punishment and nothing else. It was not quite the attitude to be building three days before the first Test. Once it was over, we all shuffled back to the hotel with our tails between our legs, our spirits very low, and our respect for our coach in question. Moss Keane, who was suffering from concussion and should have been in bed, could not finish the session and retired early. Realizing Moss's problem, I said to John Dawes that, if necessary, I would play with painkillers and padding. His reply was simple. 'You'll have to. There's no alternative.'

He was wrong. Bill Beaumont had just arrived from Britain as a replacement for Nigel Horton, who had broken his thumb and was going home. Beaumont was fit and, although he could have still conceivably been suffering from jet lag, he was the man to partner Allan Martin in the second row for the Test.

The next day, Thursday, we were all still physically

suffering from the previous day's marathon, but the biggest problem was that we were all mentally low. The stimulus of the forthcoming Test was nothing like as apparent as it should have been, and the general feeling was lethargic and casual instead of excited and sharp. John Dawes indicated that we were all to train twice that day – both morning and afternoon. The result was that most people, fearing a hard afternoon's session, held back somewhat in the morning. Once showered and dressed, we were advised that there would be no further training that day. There was considerable relief, but also anger because that had not been made clear to us earlier in the day.

Our defeat in the Test by 16 points to 12 was disappointing, though not disastrous. We might have turned the tables with a bit more flair, but the lack of individual inspiration in our team sucked us under. The All Blacks were there for the beating because, despite winning a colossal amount of ball, especially from the line-outs, they threatened little. Nevertheless, the pressure was all on us for the rest of the series because the All Blacks were certain to be better equipped, all round, by the second Test.

I was selected to play in the match immediately following the Test and despite still being in considerable pain I decided to give it a go. I badly wanted to play. However, I was found out during the practice scrummaging session. I could not bind properly on my second-row partner, Bill Beaumont, and when pressure was put on my shoulder, I was in agony. I gave it as good a go as possible but in the end I had to admit that the pain was too much. John Dawes was not amused when I advised him that I would have to withdraw from the team. I was not too happy about it either!

With Canterbury looming large in the build-up to the second Test, I was hawking myself around every physiotherapist possible to receive treatment in an attempt to accelerate the healing process in my shoulder, for which I was given injections of cortisone. Before the team was selected for the Canterbury game, I told John Dawes that, come hell or high water, I had to play. To my relief, he agreed.

Although the first Test was behind us, the tour party still had this 'sameness' about it. There was still no obvious Saturday XV and Wednesday XV, and although there were plenty of characters off the field, there was a dearth of them on it. No natural leaders with real presence had come forward to relieve the burden on our skipper's shoulders. Poor Phil Bennett did not have far to look for his problems.

The Canterbury game heralded a big change in all that. We knew that in order to give ourselves a morale boost in the lead-up to the second Test, we had to win. For the first time on the tour, Terry Cobner began to push his views to the forefront and he stimulated more players than just myself. He made us ask ourselves questions regarding our commitment, our cause and our desire for victory. He led us into the Canterbury game with the conviction that the rest of the tour depended on the outcome. He was right.

Thankfully, the 1971 battle at Lancaster Park, Christchurch, was not replayed. We made many mistakes during the game but in the end we were victorious by 14 points to 13. Just enough. For me the game marked a milestone in my career. If I had not played, I might just as well have gone home to Troon. I knew that my shoulder problem was going to remain with me until the end of the tour. I either got on with it and played, or caught the first plane home. I stayed.

Three minutes before the kick-off, as Cob was putting his final touches to his team talk, I slipped out of the dressing room into the doctor's room. There was the doctor with his pain-killing needle at the ready. Once the injections were administered, an enormous pad was then strapped to my shoulder for protection. The outcome had me feeling no pain but looking ridiculous. The Hunchback of Notre Dame had nothing on me.

The game was not a classic and at times we were under

'ou Beauty!' Scoring the first try of the tour for the Lions in South Africa, 1974

Murrayfield dressing-room capers after thumping England in the centenary international 1971. Despite torn ligaments I feel no pain! *Left to right:* Myself, Quintin Dunlop, Ian Frame, Nairn MacEwan, Gordon Strachan, Jock Turner, Alistair McHarg, Dunky Paterson, Billy Steele, Big Brother Peter, Arthur Brown, Chris Rea, and in front, balancing the champagne bottle, Ian 'Mighty Mouse' McLauchlan

Left: 'The Old Man' the year that Clyde FC won the Scottish Cup

Below: Enjoying the fresh sea breezes on Troon beach at six months old

Bottom: Family outing at Muirhead, Troon, in 1948. I'm the baby, hence my family nickname 'The Wee Yin'

...ht: My son Rory, aged three, and I ...ing high jinx at Troon tennis club. ...hat chance did I have, Dad?'

...ow: A night out for Linda and me — ...ly, there haven't been too many of ...se in the last few years

...tom: My daughter, Mardi (left), aged ...en, and (right) my wife Linda

Left: On top for West, against Gala, 197

Below: The big man in the line-out worl
New Zealand's Peter Whiting

Young and innocent. My debut for Scotland against South Africa, 1969. We won by 6−3. *Back row:* R. Burrell (touch judge), A.J.W. Hinshelwood, A.B. Carmichael, W. Lauder, G.L. Brown, P.K. Stagg, A.G. Biggar, J.N. Frame, I.S.G. Smith, G. McInnes (touch judge). *Front row:* I. McLauchlan, C.W.W. Rea, I. Robertson, J.W. Telfer, R.J. Arneil, F.A.L. Laidlaw, D. Paterson, M. Joseph (Wales, referee)

ove: Mike Gibson, the greatest player in the world, evading Mervyn 'Swerve' Davies, ᵉ greatest No. 8 Wales and the Lions have ever had
low: 'Oor Peter' about to dive over England's line to score at Twickenham in 1971. ᵉ first of three tries which he scored against England during his illustrious playing ᵉer

The most devastating side-step in rugby, owned by the brilliant Gerald Davies, leaves two defenders sprawling in the mud. This was the second of Gerald's four tries for the Lions against the thugs of Hawkes Bay, in 1971

The British Lions team of 1971, conquerors of New Zealand. *Back row:* C.W.W. Rea, A.J. Lewis, J.V. Pullen, A.B. Carmichael, J.F. Slattery, I. McLauchlan. *Second row:* J.P.R. Williams, J.F. Lynch, A.G. Biggar, R.B. Hiller, M.L. Hipwell, D.J. Duckham, J.C. Bevan, J. Taylor. *Third row:* J.S. Spencer, P.J. Dixon, G.L. Brown, T.M. Davies, W.J. McBride, M.G. Roberts, D.L. Quinnell, W.D. Thomas. *Front row:* G.O. Edwards F.A.L. Laidlaw, R.J. McLoughlin, Dr D.W.C. Smith (Manager), S.J. Dawes (Captain C.R. James (Assistant Manager), C.M.H. Gibson, B. John, R. Hopkins

Left: Line-out ball wasn't easily come by in New Zealand. Against Auckland, 1971

Below: The poor stag didn't stand a chance with Willie-John and me both after it

Bottom: Relaxing at the water's edge on Troon beach, reflecting on the rigours of a great tour

Above: Being introduced to Her Majesty the Queen. Also in the picture: Ian McLauchlan, Ian McGeechan and Billy Steele

Below: The 1971 Test series is ours! Looking on as the great All Blacks' Captain, Colin Meads, congratulates th Lions' 'Big Three' – Skipper John Dav Manager Doug Smith and Coach Carw James

great pressure, but in the end our determination, thanks largely to the motivation and leadership of Cob, won the day. I was happy with my play in the hurly-burly of the match. My shoulder gave me no problems whatsoever, but once the painkiller wore off, fifteen minutes after full time, I was in agony. I could not even dress myself properly. I even avoided the autograph hunters at the door of the stadium because I didn't want to be jostled.

During the game fate dealt a hand to Alex Wyllie, or 'Grizzlie' as he is nicknamed. (The 1971 Lions thought it should be 'Grisly'.) Midway through the second half, as I supported a peel round the tail of a line-out, I was grabbed by a Canterbury player and swung round crazily onto the ground. As this was happening my boot caught Wyllie a glancing blow at his knee, slicing it open and damaging the ligaments. He was led from the field never to return, to my knowledge, to top-class rugby again. To think that a few days before the game I assisted in administering treatment which allowed him to play against us. The physiotherapist who was treating me was also looking after the Canterbury players and Alex required some stretching of the spine and neck manipulation. It was I who held him firmly by the feet while the treatment was carried out. After the match I realized that my shoulder would certainly not heal much until I stopped training and playing. I resigned myself to using painkillers and padding for the rest of the tour.

Cinema visits are synonymous with long rugby tours, being the major distraction from boredom in the evenings. In 1971 I went to the cinema on average once a week. It was three times a week *minimum* in 1977. I remember seeing *A Clockwork Orange* three times in one week!

On the 1971 tour a Dracula film was the attraction one night. During the film, just as Dracula was about to sink his teeth into the unsuspecting neck of his lady friend, Ian McLauchlan jabbed two fingers into the neck of Sean Lynch, the Irish prop. Sean did not like creepy-crawly things and he did not simply jump with fright – he erupted! This transformed the main film into the supporting feature.

When we arrived at Athletic Park for the game against Wellington, I could not ignore the difference in the playing conditions compared with 1971. In 1971, the sun shone, the ground was firm, and there was not one puff of wind. We scored nine tries and they were all beauties. I have never seen such magnificent attacking play. I felt so proud, sitting in the stand, watching, to be associated with that Lions team. We attacked and counterattacked. We never let up. It was copy-book stuff from the forwards and magical flair from the backs. Wellington were anything but a poor team but we were so brilliant they could not stem the tide. It was a day when British rugby finally clicked, and I am so chuffed that I can always say 'I was there.' In 1977, the pitch was muddy, wet and heavy, the continual rain fell from black skies and the wind blew strongly down the pitch. As usual, there was a damned curtain raiser in full swing to make absolutely sure that the playing surface was a shocker.

The game was a cracker despite the conditions, and I felt afterwards that at long last I was beginning to fire on all cylinders. It was a great feeling after all the frustrations I had encountered since my sending-off six months previously. The show was on the road!

After we had trained and played in miserably wet conditions for the greater part of the tour, the Marlborough game was like a pot of gold at the end of a rainbow. It was a beautiful day, the pitch was firm and we all felt like playing. Those who were not selected were jealous. It was lovely playing in the sunshine. Moreover, I scored a try, the only one I scored during the whole tour. We won by 47 points to 23 and I think the crowd enjoyed the exchanges. I certainly did.

I was partnered by Bill Beaumont. As this game was just before the second Test, I knew that I was in with a chance of a Test place, and I reckoned that if Bill produced the goods alongside me that day, we would play in

the Test together. I told him that just before the kick-off.
He seemed modestly surprised, but said that he was going
to give it his all anyway. Midway through the second half
of a pulsating game, there was a stoppage for an injury.
Bill Beaumont was standing beside me and he said, 'I'm
shattered – I'll never make the Test team now. I've blown
it.'

I was mad at him. He was playing really well. He had to
keep going. 'If you believe that,' I squeezed out from
behind clenched teeth, 'I'll belt you one in the mouth here
and now.'

He flinched, thought for a moment, and then said, 'I'm
feeling great!' The following day we were both picked to
lock the scrum for Britain in the second Test.

The pressure was really on us for that Test. Although
we had put together five good wins since losing the first
Test we were still not clicking as a team. We still had too
many players out of form and most of us were carrying
injuries of some sort. Many of us were homesick and the
awful weather was taking its toll. We were all terribly
bored. The incessant rain made it difficult for us to get
away from the hotel in the afternoons. Plans for golfing,
sightseeing, boat trips, shooting expeditions were constantly being cancelled. It was so easy to sit down after
lunch – a big lunch at that – and have a few beers. Kicking
around the hotel listening to the rain battering against the
window led to only one thing – a few more beers. Eventually the monotony would be broken. By dinner! We would
go right through the menu. We generally ate far too much.
At night, if the cinema was not open we stayed in the hotel
– and had a few more beers. Consequently, the initial part
of the following day's training was aimed at ridding
ourselves of the effects of the previous day's indulgences.
It was a shame for the few who did not overindulge since
they still had to train.

On previous Lions tours, I had received regular invitations to people's homes for lunch or dinner. It was a
most welcome change from the hotel. But on this tour, the

invitations were few and far between. I missed them. There was nothing better than sitting down with a family in their own home and enjoying home-cooking and family patter.

In 1971 the reaction of the New Zealand press, and the population at large, to our arrival was 'Welcome, ye lambs to the slaughter.' We were not feared by our hosts in any way despite the great respect they held for many individuals in our party. The first newspaper I saw at the airport had a full front-page, face-only photograph of Colin Meads, the great All Black second-row forward. His face seemed hewn from granite and one pressman looked at me and said, 'Brownie, boy, you'll run a mile if you meet old Meadsie in the street, never mind take him on at rugby – he'll kill yer!'

We were given great welcomes wherever we went in 1971 and were continually being asked to sign auto-graphs. The biggest autograph session I've *ever* taken part in was at Palmerston North during the 1971 tour. We arrived there the day after our victory in the third Test. Our Dakota plane circled the town square a few times before landing at the nearby airport, and we could see the crowds in their thousands thronging the square. We journeyed from the airport to the town square in vintage cars, all in wonderful condition. We each had a car to ourselves with our names emblazoned on the front so that as we drove round and round the square, the public knew exactly who was inside. It was a marvellous occasion and we were given a rapturous welcome. Our cars eventually dropped us all off at the centre of the square and although the team hotel was barely 150 yards away, it took me at least two and a half hours to get to it. I signed autographs all that time!

In 1977, however, there was a generally hostile feeling towards us from the New Zealand public right from the beginning of the tour. We were, after all, the owners of the mythical 'world crown', having beaten both New Zealand and South Africa. New Zealand had also just been de-

feated in a test series in South Africa. Were we, therefore, going to put the final nail in the rugby coffin of this
proud, small country, once home of the unchallenged
world champions? The country was also still smarting
from Britain's recent involvement in the EEC and the
subsequent kick in the teeth that it meant to New
Zealand.

I was also conscious of us being hounded by the press in
a manner which I had never experienced on a tour before.
There seemed to be almost more reporters hanging about
us than actual rugby writers. We had less privacy than
ever as a consequence. This forced us to be much more
secretive, and therefore devious, in our use of what leisure
time we had.

Instead of the pressure easing the longer the tour lasted,
it increased. We grew more and more introverted as
individuals and as a team. The press and the public
generally castigated us for this.

John Dawes fought a running battle, at first with the
New Zealand press, but eventually with journalists from
Britain, and this did not help their treatment of us. Much
of what John Dawes did and said was, I believe, his way of
trying to protect the team and individuals from criticism,
but unfortunately some of his stances were extreme. He
even saw fit to abuse dreadfully some members of the
British press in the middle of his birthday celebrations –
celebrations which these pressmen had not only organized
but for which they had also provided the champagne.

Some of the press comment and criticism about our
style of play, individual form, training sessions, and off-
the-field behaviour was justified. Unfortunately, much of
it went over the top and was exaggerated, and this did
nothing to help the sagging confidence of quite a proportion of the tour party. It was therefore easy to understand the questioning which Derek Quinnell and I had to
take from our team mates. 'What on earth made you two
want to come back to this bloody island for?' This was a
standard question. Incessant rain, injuries galore, poor

form, bad press. Who could blame them? But it had not been like that in 1971.

There is one point which every member of the general public and the press should remember. Every Rugby Union player is an amateur, and he is playing the game for his own enjoyment and nothing else. A professional attitude, commitment and performance are now demanded by all. Not everyone at this level of rugby, no matter what his playing ability, can take these ever-increasing outside pressures in his stride and cope with them, as is expected, with the aplomb of a professional ambassador. The true character of some of rugby's greatest players has sometimes, on tour, been found to be not up to expectation. Should such a player be castigated for this in such a manner that it will be held against him for the rest of his life? Surely not.

4

Swimming but Drowning

The second Test was the watershed of the tour. We had to win. Defeat would have killed the tour as far as public interest in Britain was concerned and would have placed an intolerable burden on our shoulders as we sought to finish the remaining third of the tour respectably. In the dressing room before the game I felt more pressure on me than I had ever felt throughout the whole of my rugby career. In this game, survival was the operative word rather than victory. Terry Cobner had grown in stature immensely in the build-up to the Test and he was leading the pack. After Phil Bennett had delivered what I thought was a super team talk, Cob led the forwards into the shower room to add privately his bit of encouragement. His emotive words as we huddled together in the confined space created the perfect realistic reaction from us all. We felt a closeness, a brotherhood, between us which we not only took with us onto the field that day but which remained with us for the rest of the tour. He never raised his voice once as he spoke. Simple sentences struck home to us. 'The lights are coming on in the valleys' was one. He reminded us of all the rugby fanatics back home in Britain who had set their alarms to rouse them from their beds at 3.30 a.m. to listen to the radio commentary on the match. 'We must be able to look one another in the eye tonight, and every night for the rest of our lives.' A pure reference to the wonderful bond which players can generate be-tween each other on such tours. He spared us the banal requests, like 'dying for the cause'. I had a commitment second to none for the cause, but dying in the process was not in the script. Ever!

We took the field once I had had my shoulder numbed by the painkilling needle and padded with sponge. The Hunchback of Troon rode again! Ours was not a cavalier spirit, however; more a cold determination allied to a deep, passionate confidence in each other, especially within the pack.

The arena was not for the faint-hearted or the weak-willed. Restraint was not prevalent anywhere on the pitch; in fact, such was the brutality of some of the exchanges that the game was no advertisement for rugby football. Certain members of the All Blacks team seemed to have been overmotivated, namely Eveleigh, Bush and Taylor (a winger!). We wanted to win the game desperately; the All Blacks seemed to want to stop us at all costs.

I struck a major blow for my confidence at the first line-out. It was an All Blacks throw-in just inside our 25. They threw the ball to Andy Haden beside me and I outjumped him to fingertip the ball down to Brynmor Williams at scrum half. The ball was cleared to halfway and I was elated. Throughout the first half I managed to win a lot of ball and allied to the magnificent efforts of Bill Beaumont and Willie Duggan, we dominated the line-outs. This was one of the few contrasts with 1971 that I found welcome. The line-out play in New Zealand had changed drastically. In the Test matches, when I was jumping against Andy Haden, it was an enjoyable contest. We obviously made contact with each other, but I was never aware of it being a physical confrontation as had been the case in 1971 with Peter Whiting. On the other hand, maybe I was just becoming blasé about physical contact.

Our scrummaging was rock solid as well and this all produced a platform from which we could set up play. We kept the game as tight as possible which under the very heavy conditions was no bad thing. Sadly, the many excellent aspects of the forward battle were overshadowed by the brutal punch-ups and kicking matches between players. There were so many flash points to this game that I cannot remember the vast majority of them! I would have had to watch the television film to refresh my memory, but for a re-run of that game, I do not crave.

The second half was a real nailbiter. Our early lead of 13 points to nil was slowly whittled away and the Kiwis were beginning to win more and more line-out ball. I deliberately knocked throws to Haden down onto his side of the line-out into the gap between Sid Going, the scrum half, and the touchline. With our ever alert hooker Peter Wheeler bursting round the front of the line-out onto the ball, we gained ground. This tactic was to my mind more constructive than attempting to win the ball for ourselves, as we were kicking into the wind and would not have gained much more ground.

As the All Blacks slowly crept nearer – they got up to 13–9 – we were really facing an onslaught. The boiling point of tempers was reached too often, and late tackling and obstruction were commonplace. Some superb individual play was lost in the maelstrom of filth being perpetrated and the thoughts of all of the delegates present from the Pacific Rugby Congress must have been choice. Here we were, the supposed cream of two of the top rugby-playing nations of the world, dishing up an embarrassment.

Graham Price of Pontypool must be the quietest prop in the world. He hardly speaks, and even when he does what he says is short and to the point. On the rugby field his ability does all the talking for him. He is very strong and scrummages on his terms rather than an opponent's. He is extremely mobile and never hesitates to sacrifice himself for his cause. He received some brutal punishment from the All Blacks, especially Billy Bush and Ian Kirkpatrick, and finished the game in one hell of a state. I know there are two sides to every story, but his physical condition was disgraceful. One eye was closed completely, the other on its way. His jersey was in shreds and he was covered in stud marks – and still he said nothing!

We had taken the field with survival our mission, but that survival primarily meant winning the Test to keep the tour alive. Unfortunately, because of the dubious tactics immediately employed by some All Blacks, to which we certainly responded, such survival became a matter of physical necessity.

I thought the final whistle would never come. I had been back on antibiotics for another bad cold and during the last ten minutes I battled with my lungs and muscles to keep going. When the referee at long last put me out of my misery and ended the battle (another one?) of Lancaster Park, I stood still, closed my eyes and sighed to myself, 'We've done it. We've actually done it.' The relief was so overwhelming and my body was screaming at me with so much pain, I just wanted to lie down on top of the mud, curl up into a wee ball and sleep for a month. That was until somebody belted me in the back of the head. There were hundreds of spectators on the pitch, some sinking ankle deep in the mud, and one of them decided to take his frustrations out on me. Maybe he had seen me take so many punches during the game that he thought one more would not be noticed! It certainly brought me back to my senses and I found the strength to bulldoze my way through the throng to the safety of the dressing room. Once inside that haven, the battle was behind me. It was history. We were victorious in that we had scored more points. But the majority of us celebrated only modestly that night.

When we got back to the hotel, I shared the lift with Cob up to our rooms. 'Can I look you in the eye then, Cob?' I asked him.

'Broonie, boy, after today you can look me straight in the eye all night long, and every night for the rest of your life!' he said.

Terry Cobner was like John Dawes in 1971, a player's player. He did much about the field that only his team mates could fully appreciate. He received a tough wel-

come on his first visit to Murrayfield in 1975. He ended up
at the bottom of the first real ruck of the game and was
rucked right out of it along with the ball on our side. He
did not complain – he was too impressed! He impressed
me, too. I will always remember him as the man responsible for pulling us all up by the scruff of the neck as a team
during the 1977 tour.

The following morning Dod Burrell and our physio
'Doc' Murdoch roused us early from our beds and instigated a mass singsong in one of the bedrooms. It was the
relaunching of the tour. The problems of the last two
months were put firmly behind us and we were the
happiest we had been since leaving London. For four
hours at least we sang and drank whilst crammed together
in this one bedroom. It was my task as 'duty boy' that day
to break things up eventually and make sure that we all
got to the airport on time as the show rolled on to another
venue. It was not easy. We could have stayed there for
days.

The run-up to the third, and most important, Test was
filled with drama and excitement, and even some sunshine! There was a rousing game against the Maoris
which we eventually won after seemingly being out of it
completely. Our backs, relishing the sunshine, produced
the goods to ensure victory.

More sunshine greeted us at Waikato and lifted our
spirits tremendously. The bus journey to the ground from
our hotel was very short and we arrived at the dressing-
room door while still only halfway through our team song,
'Country Road'. No one moved a muscle while we sang on
and on. The spectators all must have been wondering
what the heck we were up to. We had no sooner hit the last
note when Terry Cobner jumped to his feet and shouted to
us, 'Come on, lads, we're here to beat them at rugby, not
scare them to death with our bloody singing.'

We had Bobby Windsor propping against Waikato. It
was a daft choice, despite Bob's talents. Phil Orr, the
Irishman, who for some stupid reason was not all that

75

popular with most of the team, should have been selected at tight-head instead, even though he normally played loose-head. I do not believe that Phil did not want to play. It was a daft game anyway. We never settled and, despite the lovely conditions and scoring three tries, we played poorly as a unit, wasting a mountain of possession.

Clive Williams, the loose-head prop, was the victim of one of the worst cases of injury diagnosis of all time. He damaged his knee and despite attempting to continue, he had to admit defeat, and in agony left the field for attention. He soon reappeared because the local New Zealand doctor said that his knee was OK. At the next scrum it was obvious to me that Clive was in dire straits and I told him to go off immediately.

'But the doctor won't let me,' he replied, quite distressed.

'It is *your* bloody knee,' I shouted at him. 'Just tell him there's no way you can continue.'

He went off and Phil Orr came on as substitute. Clive never played again on tour. He had ruptured a medial ligament and was operated on in hospital within days.

The New Zealand Juniors match, back in wet, windy, muddy Wellington, was a disgrace. The conditions were so bad the players were endangered. The match was played for one reason and one reason only – profiteering! The New Zealand Rugby Union should hang its head in shame for having allowed this match – which was of little importance – to be played. I thank God that I was not selected to play. Imagine *me* not wanting to play for the British Lions! I was on the substitutes' bench and late on in the game, when all the players were so caked in slimy mud that identification was almost impossible, Allan Martin indicated to me that he was going to come off. He had spied me laughing at something one of the other substitutes had said and thought that I was laughing at him. I pleaded with him from my vantage point to stay on and his white teeth gleamed as he gave me a devilish grin – he knew that he had me squirming! He did not come off. That bit of humour aside, it was a degrading experience, for all the players.

A victory over the might of Auckland (in sunshine!) gave us a great boost for the third Test a week later. Our power in the pack set the seal on the game and I tremendously enjoyed my joust with the giant Andy Haden in the line-outs. The score of 34 points to 15 reflected perfectly the flow of the game and all six of our tries came directly from scrummage situations. Willie Duggan, our battling and irrepressible number eight, scored from his pick-up of our ball as we drove over the line following a 5-yard scrum. The scrum position was midway between the posts and the right-hand touchline. He was to attempt the same thing in the last few seconds of the final Test, with catastrophic results.

We pulverized the All Blacks pack in the third Test. We annihilated them in the scrums, dominated them in the line-outs, overpowered them in the mauls and out-rucked them generally. The result? We lost. Never have I witnessed so much possession wasted and kicked away. Our backs seemed unable to produce any attacking moves whatsoever and were devoid of ideas. We in the forwards must shoulder some blame, nevertheless. We had enough control of the ball we were winning to take it on again and again before laying it back to the outsides for execution. Instead, we were too much like a sausage machine and we continually passed the buck to our skipper, Phil Bennett, who had plenty of problems of his own, and not many solutions. We had chances galore – even kicks in front of the posts – but squandered the majority of them. If ever there was an All Blacks team there for the beating it was this one, despite the fact that they scored a try in the first minute.

When Douglas Morgan came on as a substitute in the second half for Brynmor Williams, he was astounded at the sausage-machine rut that we were in up front. We were a magnificent ball-winning pack but we were also most boring! However, to this day I still do not know how we

77

managed to lose the Test by 19 points to 7. However, there was one major improvement in this match in which both teams shared equally, Conduct. There was not one unpleasant incident during the whole game.

Brynmor's tour was over and the replacement was not Gareth Edwards, as we had all hoped, but Alan Lewis, a London Welshman. 'Fatty' Lewis was his affectionate nickname. Although we were disappointed that Gareth had turned down the opportunity to join us, I felt that some of my team mates went over the top with their reaction to the news that Alan was joining us instead. The great majority of the comments came from the Welshmen. 'Bloody London snob. Toffee-nosed idiot. Bighead. Takes nothing seriously.' These were just a few of the utterings. The comments were so many and varied that those who did not know Alan were decidedly against him before he arrived. I could not believe it. We had been away from the realistic wide world too long and all of our thoughts were now clouded. It was something which I had suspected for some time. At Christchurch airport before the third Test, Andy Haden had called me from the team bus to give me a holdall for my training kit (this was the outcome of a conversation I had with Andy following the Auckland match). Some of my team mates' reactions to my fraternization with Andy were pathetic.

We picked up Alan Lewis from the airport on our way by bus to play North Auckland. He bounced onto the bus full of the joys of spring, looking as if he had just been presented with a million pounds. My team mates hardly mirrored him! He plonked himself down in a seat near the front of the bus and our journey continued. After watching Alan sitting on his own for some time I moved down beside him. I filled him in on the developments of the tour and asked what the weather was like back home in Britain which, by this stage of the tour, seemed like a million miles away. He innocently glanced out the bus window and exclaimed, 'Just like here. Brilliant!'

He caused quite a stir at the training session two hours

later. First, he refused to participate in a shortened line-out move in which he was called upon to run on to a long throw over the top. 'I didn't come all this way to be killed,' was his realistic comment. Second, during our scrum practice he broke up a scrum to deliver a few tips to the pack about feet placement and ball channelling. He was not joking either. Some of the boys were blazing at his impudence. I marvelled at his honest audacity. After all, weren't we supposed to be the greatest scrummagers ever? 'He'll get his come-uppance against Sid Going on Saturday,' was one remark made later. But not a bit of it. Alan played bloody well against Sid and was very much involved in our victory by 18 points to 7 over North Auckland. That match was our last real hurdle before the fourth Test. He also turned out to be one of the most cheery, chirpy members of the whole party. We could have done with him joining us a bit earlier in the tour! Both Phil Bennett and John Bevan enjoyed his length of pass too.

The night before the North Auckland game I was sleeping in my bedroom when I was awakened by a noise at my window. Two intruders were attempting to break into my room and the first one was almost right inside! I yelled at him and he immediately began clambering back out again screaming to his accomplice, 'He's awake! He's awake!' In the pitch darkness I could not find my rugby boots to belt him with, but I did quickly fill the litter bin with boiling water from the sink and, as they fled down the fire escape, the water cascaded all over them. They dived into a car and sped off into the night, but not before I crashed the litter bin off the front windscreen. I did not sleep too soundly after that!

The evening after the North Auckland victory we spent some hours in an Italian restaurant by courtesy of our liaison officer Peter Wild, a lovely man. We had a monumental evening. The food was superb, the wine abundant and the singing hearty. It was as if we had just won the Test series. Unfortunately I was quickly sobered when Willie Duggan quite innocently pulled my right arm behind by shoulder as I leant backwards to pass some wine to his table. The searing pain in my shoulder almost made me black out. I broke into a cold sweat. Poor Willie Duggan was beside himself with concern and was very relieved, as were quite a few of my team mates, when eventually the pain began to subside. One player, who shall remain nameless, even said to me, 'And to think that some of us thought that your shoulder wasn't that bad!'

On the eve of the Bay of Plenty game I decided to have my final celebration before the final Test five days later. I was not involved at all with the Bay of Plenty game and was therefore not too early into my bed, having spent a lager-dominated evening with some team mates in similar circumstances. On the morning of the match I travelled to the local school with John Dawes and six or seven team mates for indoor training. The training was quite strenuous without being dire. Nevertheless, because of my late night, I went straight to bed to sleep as soon as we got back to the hotel. Imagine my horror when John Dawes came into my room one hour later and told me, 'Get to the dining room immediately for some lunch. Allan Martin's called off. You're playing.' The bedraggled human specimen which greeted the stares of my team mates in the dining room could not have been a very great confidence-booster. In the dressing room at the stadium before the match the usual good luck wishes to me were replaced by comments like 'Just do what you can' and 'Even if you just push in the scrum.' Guess what – I had a great game! My line-out play, which must have been pure instinct, was spot-on and I won as much ball as came my way.

The final Test broke my heart. We dominated every phase of the forward battle so decisively that it seemed almost unreal. We had a monopoly of possession and kept the game very tight and the ball at all times close to the forwards. What a sad reflection on our backs and their collective ability that they could not convert that possession into a match-winning score.

We only led by 9 points to 3 at half time. On two occasions early in the second half the All Blacks were reduced to using only three men in their scrum! I had encountered this tactic at home, playing for West of Scotland when the opposition had no answer to our domination in the scrum, but I never thought for one moment that I would witness it at Test level. It was a great boost for us psychologically even though they did manage cheekily to scramble the ball clear.

We relaxed our tight grip too early. With a few minutes remaining and the score at 9 points to 6, our concentration seemed to sag just enough for unforced errors to creep into our play and put us under pressure. We missed two very kickable penalties, they missed one. In injury time they scored a try after basic errors on our part. Ten points to 9 for them! I could not believe it. However, there were still a few minutes of injury time remaining according to the referee and we fought our way to a line-out position just short of their line. They knocked the ball over their own line and Bill Beaumont dived on it and scored as three All Blacks dived on top of him and the ball. Peter Wheeler and I jumped to the heavens in exultation only to plummet again when the referee shouted, 'Unsighted. Scrum five!' I swore inwardly at him and consoled myself with the thought of the options which were now open to us from the scrum.

The heel was clean, the scrum was held up and the ball was at my feet. The pushover try was all set. We were as tight as a drum and in full control, slowly shunting the whole scrum nearer the try line. We were slightly up on the right-hand side so I called for us to straighten. I permitted the ball to go from my feet gently back to Willie Duggan's to allow me to give 100 per cent to the shove. We straightened perfectly and I could see the try line beneath our front row's noses. 'We're there. We're going to score!' We had total control of the situation. 'LIONS' SCRUM SAVES SERIES' – I could see the banner headlines in the newspapers. But it was not to be. Willie Duggan

decided to try to repeat his try-scoring feat against Auckland in exactly the same position. He picked the ball up
and dived for the line. He was held up. Frantically we dug
for the ball but the referee blew and awarded another
scrum 5. I was seething at Willie. He did not have to pick
up and dive. We were on our way. All the way. However,
at least we had another opportunity to try again. This time
as soon as the ball hit the deck at Peter Wheeler's feet the
All Blacks front row took one great nosedive into the
ground to make the pushover impossible. Technically, of
course, it should have been a penalty try to us but there
was no way the home referee, Mr Millar, of Otago, would
have given such a decision – especially under these circumstances. We had to release the ball to the backs and as
Andy Irvine joined in the line he dropped the ball – just as
he had done at the final move of the final training session
the day before. The referee blew for full time and the series
was lost.

All the way back to the dressing room I was surrounded
by spectators – but there was nobody punching me this
time. I was numb to their jubiliation. In fact, I was numb
to the world. After congratulating the All Blacks players
and commiserating with my own team mates, I made my
way up to the main stand for the traditional final farewell
of a tour. I did not take in much of what was being said in
the short speeches. Too much was flashing through my
mind. The sending-off. My selection. The rain. The mud.
My shoulder. Hostility on and off the field. Our dominance of the All Blacks forwards in the third and fourth
Tests. Our disappointing back play. I returned to reality
to hear the traditional rendering of 'Now Is the Hour'
from the massed Eden Park crowd. It is always a very
emotional part of rugby touring and may it continue for
eternity, but it did not, and could not, divorce me from the
sickening disappointment.

My vow to myself on arriving in New Zealand – 'No
matter how the tour finishes, I must be a success' – faded
into insignificance in the light of the outcome to the Test

series. Despite feeling satisfied that I had contributed to the successful part of the tour, I was still very disappointed at losing. So many people had tried so hard for so little return that any personal glory I felt washed thin.

Although my contribution to the first half of the tour was poor in that I only played in four and a half matches out of the first thirteen, I felt that I went some way to redeeming myself by playing in nine of the remaining twelve, including the last three Tests. When I took the field for the third Test my record for Test matches on Lions tours was: played six, won five, drawn one. The defeat that day, together with the fourth Test defeat, made a sad dent in my proud record!

The final game of the tour was against Fiji, in Fiji. At least we knew that the sun would be shining there! As our plane lifted off the runway at Auckland airport the majority of my team mates let out a loud cheer that told its own story. I was certainly ready for home, deeply disappointed, but I was not bitter. After all, I had to take the rough with the smooth. My two previous flights home from Lions tours had been with victory tucked under the belt.

I can well remember Willie John McBride saying to me as we flew home from New Zealand in 1971, 'Brownie, you've been very lucky indeed to taste victory on your very first Lions tour. Take some advice from me – don't go on any more tours, because there will never be another like it.' I appreciated that victory was sweet and had to be savoured, but it obviously meant so much more to Willie because of the defeats he had suffered on his three previous Lions tours.

Having ignored his advice (as he did!), I ventured to South Africa in 1974 with the Lions where once again the result was a triumph for Britain. On the return journey from Johannesburg Willie said to me, 'Take my advice, there really will never be another tour like this one – don't push your luck!'

Did I push my luck? I do not think so. To tour with the

British Lions is the greatest reward any British player can receive. Despite my mental problems before the tour the honour of being selected was undiminished. As an amateur I relished the opportunity to be able to devote my time fully to Rugby football. To train every day, and play regularly, with the best in British rugby stimulated me immensely. I loved the banter, the rivalry, the fun, and most of all the challenge. I revelled in eating, sleeping, drinking, talking rugby and donating as much time to it as was necessary. I hated losing, but that is part of growing up.

The game against Fiji was a fiasco. Here we were relaxing and enjoying ourselves with no more pressure from statistics, press, public, telephone calls, or rain. We were stiff, sore and tired after New Zealand and the last thing any of us wanted to do was to play against big, strong, fast and elusive Fijians and on a pitch like concrete. Ten members of our party were officially declared unfit for consideration. When the team was announced, the members started hunting about for kit to wear. Our stock had been decimated since leaving New Zealand. I gave Allan Martin my shorts and socks, even though I was a substitute.

We turned out in a dreadful state. Shorts which were anything but white, jerseys which were mainly burst and grubby, socks full of holes and faded. As both teams lined up to be introduced to the Governor General of the island, the comparison was embarrassing. The Fijians looked immaculate. Pure white jerseys, jet-black shorts, black and white socks. Every one of them stood proudly erect, showing off a mass of rippling muscles like so many Olympic athletes, and just a hint of expectant perspiration gleaming on their brows. We stood like half-shut knives, bleary eyed, disorderly and uninterested. If a complete stranger had walked into the arena to be told that one of the world's top sides was to play the locals, there is no way he would have guessed which was which correctly!

We lost the game! The Fijians played with the exuberance and flair we feared they might, scoring some quite magnificent tries in the process. We battled away, driving and scrummaging them into the ground at times, but really it was never going to be our day. The final score of 25 points to 21 reflected the exciting occasion nicely. As a full-blooded international match, it was a non-starter. Their scrummaging, rucking and mauling were technically awful, but my goodness how they made up for it in the loose when they had the ball in their hands! The referee was such a joke that it was actually funny. Somehow he seemed in character with the occasion. A penalty count against us of 22 to 4 summed up his view of the game perfectly.

Late in the second half I had to substitute for Trevor Evans at wing forward. I had always fancied a game in the back row but this was hardly the one I would have chosen. I was sitting on the substitutes' bench at the halfway line and Fiji had just scored their second last try, when Trevor limped off. The conversion attempt was held up to allow me to come to the field. What a sight I must have made! I had on a pair of size 32-inch shorts which were so tight that I could not tuck in my jersey. My jersey was so long that my tiny shorts were completely hidden from view. I had on a pair of my own everday ankle socks. To kill it all, my Achilles tendon was very painful and I had to limp the first twenty yards or so to get it going. Slowly but surely it began to ease but as I crossed the 25-yard line one of my team mates standing behind the goalposts yelled out, 'Never mind, Broonie, by the looks of it we'll be better off without you!' I have it on good authority that my appearance was quite ridiculous.

The delirium which greeted the Fijians match-winning try and the referee's final whistle confirming victory was a joy to behold. This, for me, was not a defeat of real significance but a marvellous example of what hands-across-the-sea rugby is all about. As we left the field, we were cheered loudly. The swarming, jubiliant masses swept me to the team bus – a rickety, windowless contraption. It was parked next to the Fijian players' bus and I eagerly sought out the Fijian player with the cleanest and least damaged jersey and offered to do a swap. You would have thought that I had offered him a million dollars. As we headed back to the hotel, still in our gear, we were cheered all the way. It seemed as though everyone on the island knew 'the Lions are here'. What a lovely boost to our morale with which to end the tour.

We were firmly put in our place at the dinner that night. We sang a couple of songs, and were then followed by the Fijian team. They were superb. We did not sing any more but were glad just to listen.

Before leaving Fiji, I had time for a round of golf at the Pacific Harbour Golf Club with Mike Gibson, John Bevan and Alan Lewis. It was not a boring round! On the first tee, John Bevan had a big practice swing and the club flew out of his grasp into the nearby jungle – never to be found. He then hit his ball up the middle of the fairway, only to hook it with his second strike right into the jungle. How's that for an easy start? After only two blows he was already down one club and one ball. He shrugged his shoulders and said, 'Things can only improve.'

Alan Lewis replied, 'Well you've got thirteen clubs and eight balls still to go.'

Halfway round the course I crashed the two-seater buggy in which Mike Gibson and I were travelling. As it tipped over I was thrown clear but Mike was trapped, almost jammed under it, as it careered downhill at a crazy angle. I got the fright of my life and when Mike finally scrambled clear I was very relieved. He exclaimed, 'After all I've been through in New Zealand' – he was dogged by continual bad luck – 'please, God, let me survive a round of golf in Fiji.'

Fiji was lovely: hot sticky days, drinks by the poolside, beautiful food, super golf courses, happy people. Fran Cotton summed up the feelings of us all by saying, 'The Four Home Unions have got it all wrong, you know. We should have spent three months here and four days in New Zealand!'

When we had returned to Britain in 1971 over 2500 people welcomed us, along with the television cameras. It was overwhelming. Thereafter, we were wined, dined and fêted for months on end. It was an unreal world – but I liked it! On our return in 1977 there were only a handful of rugby diehards to welcome us, along with some of the players' wives. Thereafter, the tour was dead – nobody wanted to know us!

5

After the Tide's Out

Looking back on the 1977 tour, I realize that there had been quite a change in attitude in the players, compared with my other two tours. Nowhere was this change more apparent than over the question of players receiving cash and equipment and other favours. It was almost as if each player was a miniature businessman in his own right. I sensed a feeling of 'What's in it for me?' when some of the players were talking about the tour and the future prospects. I sensed this even before we left London.

A classic example of this happened two thirds of the way through the tour when we were asked if we fancied recording an LP as a souvenir. I was asked immediately by five or six other players, mostly Welsh, how much we were to be paid. I was astounded at this but nevertheless, in my capacity as choir master and therefore negotiator between ourselves and EMI, I attempted to extract some cash from them. They laughed at me.

With no money forthcoming, the players generally were reluctant to record the LP. I was amazed. I was also very angry. However, we did eventually record some songs. The recording evening was a bit of a shambles and I take my hat off to EMI for what they finally did produce, though there was never any danger of it making the charts. Amazingly enough, when the time came for the LP to be delivered to my room in the hotel, the first six or seven people into the room to pick up their copy were the players who said under no circumstances were they going to be recorded if they weren't getting paid for it. Some of the players actually spent more time attempting to line their pockets with cash, and they put more effort into that, than they ever did on the training paddock.

Maybe if they had buckled down in training the tour might have been totally different for many of them. Who knows, the outcome of the whole tour may have been altered. I certainly witnessed much more selfishness during this tour than on any other previous one and this attitude did not help the team effort. Perhaps this selfishness was brought about because the players wanted to achieve more comfort for themselves during the tour. Let's face it, there weren't many other comforts to be had. The weather for at least two thirds of the tour was absolutely diabolical. We were training in wet conditions. Our gear was always wet and needing to be washed. Training sessions never seemed to go as well, and playing and training in such wet conditions for so long affected everyone's morale. This shone through quite clearly in our play and in our attitude towards the various games. A large part of the tour was a drudgery. Because of the weather, there were too few opportunities to enjoy leisure activities. No matter how many social entertainments the liaison officer of the local rugby union attempted to lay on for us, they always seemed to be cancelled because of the rain. Boredom and homesickness grew like a cancer within the team. Little things bugged us enormously. Niggling injuries got worse by the hour. Team members who were pains became bigger pains because you couldn't get away from them. In 1971 there were natural differences of opinion and habits within the team, but because we were successful and because we had plenty of leisure activities, these things never seemed to bother us. The secret was that you could always get away from them. In 1977 on the other hand they were thrust down your throat and became major problems.

There was also much more gossiping amongst the players about one another in 1977 than there ever was in 1971. This was an aspect of the 1977 tour which I hated.

And yet when we were all in our team room drinking a few beers and singing a few songs, we enjoyed ourselves. In fact sometimes we had an absolute ball. The longer the tour went on the more we seemed to crave our own company. Certainly we craved our own company more than we craved that of the public. We became much too introverted.

We suffered many more injuries in 1977 than we ever had in 1971. This had a debilitating effect on the whole team, and not just on the players who were actually injured. During the whole of the 1977 tour there never seemed to be a set first team and subsequently we never seemed to settle into any pattern or style of play. In fact the longer the tour progressed and the more the forwards dominated the opposition, the worse our back play became and the more we lost our way. Surely never has any team squandered so much excellent possession any time, anywhere.

The saddest part of it all was the fact that we were so devoid of ideas of direction outside the scrum. Our forward performances generally were quite magnificent. They were much better than those of the 1971 pack. We totally dominated the opposition in 1977 in a way we never could in 1971. The All Blacks test pack of 1971 would have beaten the All Blacks test pack of 1977 but not in the same way we did.

Too many of our players were out of form and far too many of them lacked sparkle. In some games we played as if we were beating our heads against a brick wall. The team lacked the flair and brilliance that was so apparent in the 1971 tour. When we did get some firm grounds and some sunshine near the end of the tour, our backs showed glimpses of what could have been possible had conditions been better, but it remains a sad fact that our back division could not hold a candle to the 1971 team.

Phil Bennett battled with his fitness, form and captaincy throughout the tour. He certainly never recovered full fitness after being injured in a collision with Willie

Duggan during the first Test. The hellish, wet, muddy conditions did not suit his normal style of play, either. Unfortunately, we did not have the personnel in our back division to take the weight off Phil. I was always aware that our tactical options in the backs seemed very limited. Not only that, I cannot remember any particular style of play being decided upon or even sought. Phil Bennett is a very sensitive and somewhat introverted human being. He was all too aware of the ills, boredom and homesickness of many of the players. He was feeling exactly the same. He gave many rousing team talks which spoke volumes for the depth of feeling he had for the game and for his fellow players, but unfortunately he could not lift his own game as an inspiration either to himself or to his team mates. The All Blacks deserve credit for that. Thanks to J. J. Stewart, they knew Benny's weaknesses and how to attack them. For most of the tour, Benny seemed to be carrying the weight of the world's problems on his shoulders. There was probably no one in the team more delighted to set foot back in Britain than Benny. As a captain, he did not command the same respect as John Dawes in 1971 or Willie John McBride in 1974. He seemed completely overwhelmed and dominated by John Dawes. We all felt sorry for him, and should have loved to have done something to ease his burden. Many of us felt that he should not have been selected for the last Test and that John Bevan should have played stand-off instead, though I appreciate that this would have been the last straw as far as Benny was concerned. Still, John Bevan was an excellent all-round footballer and he had had a very good tour. He must count himself unlucky not to have played in that last Test. On playing merit, he certainly deserved to.

Having said all that, I must still add that Phil was a rare wee player. For someone with such a small build, he possessed the widest side-step I have ever seen. A shy, likeable man, he expressed himself far more by his actions on the field than he ever did verbally off it. His sad

91

experience as captain pales into insignificance when set against all that he has given to rugby by his regular demonstrations of his individual brand of brilliant, gifted football. We have many sparkling memories to thank him for, but in particular for his initiating the wonderful move which led to Gareth Edwards diving over the All Blacks try line in that memorable game with the Barbarians in 1973. The 1974 Lions remember him for some breathtaking running too. Benny's brand of attacking flair was much more suited to broken-play situations than to set pieces, despite the unforgettable try he scored from scrum possession at Ayr in 1979 when playing for my international XV. His run, from inside his own half, included countless side-steps, dummies, feints and jinks. It was lovely to hear the number of 'Ahs' of appreciation which came from the crowd.

There was one great bonus on the 1977 tour, and that was Bill Beaumont at lock. His performance was the best I have experienced from a second-row partner at Test level in three Lions tours. That is why I would unhesitatingly nominate Bill to lock the scrum with me in my ideal team drawn from British Lions of the 1970s. Bill won cleanly virtually every line-out ball that was thrown to him; he plundered or destroyed all the ball thrown to his opponent Frank Oliver. He scrummaged like a demon, rucked and mauled as though his life depended on it, and trained and played with an enthusiasm that inspired me. How ironic that he should only have been given the chance to demonstrate this as a sixth-choice lock in Britain in the estimation of the Lions tour selection committee.

He played at all times fairly and cleanly, and epitomized the conviction that a player can be a hard, driving forward, winning respect from friend and foe alike, without being at all dirty. Bill's enforced premature retirement has robbed the game of one of its finest playing ambassadors. A great lump of a man, he enhanced the game's dignity and appeal by his natural and unassuming manner while riding the crest of the wave as England's skipper.

92

I doubt if he will ever start to understand his popularity, which stretches far beyond the borders of Lancashire and England.

Roger Uttley is the same sort of man. He always did his job properly, grafting selflessly at all times, and we missed him dreadfully in 1977 in New Zealand. His ball-winning ability and tactical mind would have given our back row the impetus we needed to launch back-row moves, especially in the third and fourth Tests. With Roger in our back row, I think we would have saved the series and might even have won it.

6

Mauling Springboks

The peaks of my rugby career were undoubtedly my three tours with the British Lions. In that I was extremely lucky. Most players would count themselves fortunate even to have made one Lions tour. It has been said, with enough of an element of truth in it to goad me into defending myself, that I only realized my full potential as a rugby footballer on those Lions tours, and that I did not give as much when playing for any other team. There is an element of truth in that, but again I would remind critics that Rugby Union footballers are amateur players. When they are at home, they live the lives of amateurs. They have to earn a living and most of them get married and have families and, quite properly, those activities have to take precedence. Playing rugby is something that is done, and done gladly, in one's spare time. It has to take third or fourth place in a man's life.

On tour, however, that does not apply. On tour, a Rugby Union footballer lives the life of a professional player. His full-time job is practising and playing rugby, and furthering the advance of the game through social contacts. I do not deny that this is an enjoyable exercise. I will go further and say that it is absolutely bloody marvellous. I enjoyed the experience not only because of the places I visited and the friends I made but because at the same time I found out my full potential as a rugby player. That would not have been possible in other circumstances, and that is why I think it is quite wrong to point a finger at a player and upbraid him because he does not

94

achieve the same standards when he is playing as a part-timer as he does when he plays full time. Why are there such differences between top-class professional soccer players and the rest? The reason is exactly the same.

Participating in a major tour is unique so far as a rugby footballer is concerned. Each tour is different, as I saw in New Zealand in 1971 and 1977. There could have been no greater contrast between the two, even though they took place in the same country. One was a triumph; the other a disaster. One was pure exhilaration; the other sheer misery. Both of them, though, taught me things about myself, about my fellow players and about the game that I had not known before.

As I have said, much of the contrast between the 1971 and 1977 tours had to do with the weather, the different training and playing conditions, and the consequent difference in leisure activities. Well, there is one place on this earth where rugby footballers never have to worry about the weather, and that is South Africa. There the sun nearly always shines. The grounds are nearly always dry. The training facilities are as good as the food and the wine, and the variety of scenery and leisure activities is breathtaking. If you cannot play rugby there, you cannot play it anywhere.

South African rugby was at a low ebb in 1974. They had not played a Test series for four years, and that is at least half a playing generation. I know how much I missed not playing for half a season, so I can fully appreciate what that gap meant to the Springboks.

The tour had been opposed by the usual people, mostly, it seemed at the time, from overseas, who wanted to use sport as a way of voicing their political objections to South Africa. Happily, the Four Home Unions were not deterred and went ahead. The protestors even provided us with a quite unexpected bonus. Their threats of disruption and civil disobedience persuaded the Four Home Unions to dispense with the usual week of training and preparation at Eastbourne – the week that had dragged so threateningly in 1971 – and instead they decided that we should fly straight to South Africa and spend the extra week training there. The full benefits of arriving as soon as possible in the host country were quickly discovered by us and we made the most of them.

I am a firm believer in building bridges between countries, and I think rugby is going to play an increasing role in international relationships. I am sure that the breaking of sporting links between countries because of differing political viewpoints is retrograde, an act that should only happen between countries at war.

There are plenty of countries in which many things take place of which I do not approve, but that does not make me feel that sporting links should be cut, especially when other links such as trade, business, banking, insurance and tourism are still regarded as not only acceptable but desirable. Obviously sport is up front for everyone to see; it cannot be hidden under the carpet as other things can, but so long as these other connections exist, then I am all for maintaining sporting connections too.

I am appalled at religious bigotry, political prisoners, apartheid and suppression of free speech, but I cannot see that maintaining links with countries which have these intolerances indicates approval. We all live in glass houses of one sort or another.

From the point of view of rugby pure and simple, for me the 1974 tour had everything. Great victories, great weather, magnificent leisure opportunities and, to cap it all, I played as well as I have ever done, before or since. Our pack was superb. Each member complemented the rest. We had height, weight, mobility and technique that were unmatched by anything the Springboks could manufacture. Our back division did the job that was asked of it, although without the overall élan and individual brilliance of the 1971 backs. Still, they ran in some magnificent scores, especially in the Tests. This was something that not even the 1971 backs could achieve at Test level.

Willie John McBride dominated as captain. He had the respect of every team member and he dove-tailed perfectly with the team coach Syd Millar. Together they were the architects of a fabulous Test series victory.

The Springboks' lack of match practice at international level inevitably meant that some of their forwards were rusty. Some of the other forwards just did not come up to scratch at all. In the third Test I played against two lock forwards, 'Moaner' van Heerden and Johan de Bruyn, neither of whom could really jump. I loved it. Their lack of technique and skill was astounding. All they had was a physical presence. Bruises heal eventually so they really did not cause me any great problems.

The line-outs in South Africa were nothing like the all-in wrestling fiascos I had encountered in New Zealand in 1971. Nevertheless, each line-out still required a fair amount of physical commitment, especially when I was jumping against the massive John Williams who stood 6 feet 10 inches tall. I could not allow him too many clear jumps at the ball!

I found the scrummaging in South Africa in 1974 far less demanding than either 1971 or 1977 in New Zealand. This of course gave me much more energy to run about in the loose and enabled me to be more far-ranging with my support play than I had ever been in New Zealand. The magnificent playing conditions in South Africa also made the game more open. It seemed to suit my style of play, too, because I have never enjoyed myself as much on any tour as I did in South Africa. The South African backs were generally boring and unimaginative but nevertheless I felt that they still had more to offer than the 1971 New Zealand backs.

Our first game in South Africa was against Western Transvaal at Potchefstroom. I was very fit and raring to go. I was to play opposite the local 'monster', 6 foot 6 inch Jan Tromp, who had featured prominently in the pre-match psyching. He was rough, tough and strong, according to the local newspaper. I was advised, quite firmly, to keep out of his way all afternoon. What with this and the reported goings-on in the corresponding fixture in the previous Lions tour in 1968, during which many Lions were battered and injured, I approached the contest with a certain caution.

When we arrived at the stadium we had to walk along the side of the pitch in front of the main stand to gain access to the dressing rooms. We received the most un-believable reception from the crowd. I was quite over-whelmed by it. Even the curtain-raiser match came to a temporary halt. Mind you, one hour later, when we emerged from the dressing room into the brilliant sun-shine to launch the tour, the reception was rather different – we now represented 'the enemy within' and were looked upon as such. That impression was to stay with me throughout the whole tour.

My tour got off to a cracking start. The match was barely five minutes old when I supported a bullocking run by wing forward Tommy David. He was floored ten yards short of the line, but still managed to throw the ball one-handed to me. It was very low, below knee height, but I managed to take it in my stride and dive over the line to score the first try of the tour. It was the first try of nine that we scored in that match and we gave a magnificent display of fast, open, running rugby off a solid forward base – and I loved every single minute of it.

Jan Tromp never bothered me. Late in the game, when they tried a short penalty routine near our line, Jan Tromp was obviously going to be the man erupting with the ball, and accordingly, we were ready. We halved him! The tour had started very well both for me and for the team, and I was determined to do my best to keep it that way.

By the time we came to play Transvaal at Ellis Park, I had played in seven out of nine matches, and the Trans-vaal game was to be my fifth in succession. I certainly wasn't getting a chance of becoming bored.

As soon as we arrived in our hotel in Johannesburg, I

went straight to bed. I was suffering from flu and was put into isolation in case I spread germs about. Some others in our party were similarly affected. Ken Kennedy, the doctor, was the only person I saw for two days, and I'm grateful to him for his patience and medications. I trained on the Friday, and although weak and slightly dizzy, I declared myself fit to play.

The sight of Ellis Park, Johannesburg, took my breath away completely. The terraces were so steep and high that I wondered how the aircraft flying over the city managed to avoid them. The stadium held 70,000 spectators, few of whom were cheering for us.

The home supporters had plenty to cheer about because it looked as though Transvaal were going to become the first team to lower our colours. By half time they were leading by 9 points to 3 and their enormous pack was proving quite a handful. At least six of my team mates had also been in bed with flu during the previous week and some had not even been well enough to train on Friday. What with that, the altitude, and the pride of Transvaal, it was all uphill in the second half. We knuckled down, threw off the effects of the flu, acclimatized to the thin air and, as Willie John would say, 'We got the show on the road.'

We displayed magnificent team spirit, guts and determination, and came back with a bang. Those 70,000 people were on the edge of their seats as the score hung in the balance at 16 points to 15 in our favour with only a few minutes remaining. It was Tony Neary who scored a marvellous try to seal our victory. The game had been hard, uncompromising, but fair. The true spirit of top-class rugby football had been on full display and I was proud to have been part of it.

Exactly one week later, the Lions went to Pretoria to play South Africa in the second Test. The atmosphere in the Loftus Versveld stadium was tense and expectant. Sixty-three thousand spectators were crammed together in anticipation of a mammoth clash of forward power and rugby skills. They were not disappointed!

As I ran onto the field, I took in as much of the atmosphere as possible. Before the kick-off, with my heart pounding, I thought to myself, 'This is the real big time – and I love it.' As in the first Test, we immediately settled into our scrummaging and from that solid base began the demolition of the South Africans. I renewed my battle in the line-out with big John Williams. He was still smarting from the poor press he had received after the first Test and was obviously in no mood for frivolity. The first time I challenged him he belted me one on the jaw – and it was sore! I honestly thought that my jaw was broken, and by the way he was looking at me, I am sure he thought it was too! Thankfully, it was not.

Despite the pressure, the game was generally played in a good spirit, just as the first Test had been, and at a fast and furious pace. Although not dominating, we neverthe-less played with great confidence – particularly Gareth Edwards and Phil Bennett, our halfbacks. Phil was at his best, running from deep defensive situations, and it was one of these, after half an hour's play, that produced a try for J. J. Williams, his second of the match. Phil ran out of our 25 at top speed and, after the ball passed between four or five players, including me, J.J. burst onto it and sprinted over the line, with me right next to him just in case.

That try gave us a half-time lead of 10 points to 3, thanks to Gerald Bosch, the Springboks stand-off, being off target with quite a few kicks at goal. In the second half we gradually took control of the forward exchanges and this in turn encouraged the backs to be more adventurous, particularly Phil Bennett. Early in the second half he ran fully fifty yards, dodging, weaving and side-stepping, on the way to scoring a wonderful try. That took us to 14 points to 6, a comfortable margin but not conclusive. However, I scored a try not long after which took the score up to 18 points to 6 and sealed the game for us. I supported a touch-line charge by Gareth after he had fielded an attempted touch kick from fullback McCallum. He was stopped ten yards short of the line, but hearing my call on the inside, popped the ball up into my path. Despite the close attentions of some Springboks, nothing was going to stop me. I ploughed to the line to dive over triumphantly for my fifth try of the tour. Boy, was I delighted! A few minutes later, I put cream on top of my cake when I outjumped the massive John Williams, and Ian McGeechan duly dropped a goal from the possession.

J. P. R. Williams awarded me one big black mark before the game was over. I called for, and fielded, an enormous up-and-under kick just outside our 25. As the whole Springboks pack descended on me, I swung away to the open side, and J.P.R. came up outside me screaming for a pass. I kicked the ball away – right down the throat of the Springboks wing, Germishuys. With J.P.R.'s oaths ringing in my ears, I looked outside him and saw that if I had passed the ball we would have had a three-man overlap – at least! My impetuosity had cost me a part in what would have been a famous try. I later said to J.P.R., 'I could have kicked myself for that.' He replied, 'I could have kicked you, too.'

Two up in the Test series with two matches to go meant that we went to Port Elizabeth for the third Test in the unprecedented position of needing only one more victory to win the series. Two bites at the cherry! We were confident that we would need only one.

Our build-up and preparation were perfect. The application from the whole Test side and from the rest of the tour party was 100 per cent. I realize now that when we set off for the Boet Erasmus stadium, we were going to what I will remember as the most important match of my rugby career – 'The Big Pictur' as the great Billy Hunter, of Hawick, would call it. I led the boys in song during the journey and we were all in full voice, as one.

Our feeling of togetherness oozed around the dressing room. There was no shouting or gesticulating. We all knew why we were there and what we were going to do about it. All the weeks and months of training, playing and talking had come to a head, and in the words of Willie John, 'There is no escape now.'

In the captain's bedroom three hours earlier I had become totally switched on. There were only the eight Test forwards present, and when Willie John spoke, we listened! With fifty-seven caps for Ireland and on his fifth Lions tour, he knew what he was talking about. 'Mighty, Bobby, Fran, Broonie, myself, Slatts, Swerve, Roger, it's all up to us.' His voice never rose above a whisper, he told each of us what he expected. His dedicated determination and open emotion flowed from him. Of course we all wanted to play for each other and become the first Test team in history to win a series in South Africa; but Willie John made us want it that little bit more.

Despite the intense pressure there was no great emotion displayed in the dressing room. We all had a cool, calm appreciation of the job in hand. But there was, of course, a bit of drama. Just before leaving the dressing room to take the field, Willie John marched right down the team line-up thumping each one of us on the chest, calling out each name at the same time. It was very effective in identifying every one of us with the cause. I was last in the line and braced myself for the impending blow, which was duly delivered. Unfortunately, as I relaxed, Willie John pivoted to face the whole team and hit me again, winding me. I could not concentrate properly on his final words of encouragement, I was too busy gasping for breath!

My captain's assault was a warmer-upper for me for the conflict ahead. The exchanges during the first half were brutal. Gone totally was the decent spirit of the first two Tests. It was now a battle, a physical battle. The Springboks were like men possessed, chopping anything wearing a red shirt which moved. We were being belted right, left and centre without penalty. The constant pressure we were under inside our own 25 meant that we could not retaliate for fear of giving away penalty points. With the low, dazzling sun and the breeze in our faces, we were really up against it, but survived by calling upon all our resources of pride, guts, determination, strength and ability.

Our resolve was taken beyond the limit, though, when midway through the half Van Heerden ploughed through a ruck, crazily stamping on as many of us as possible. Despite the fact that the ruck was right on our line, we retaliated. The mass punch-up which followed won no medals for any of us as amateur rugby players promoting the game of rugby football, but it showed the Springboks that we would not accept such outright thuggery, whatever the cost.

Despite winning a fair share of possession, we could not get the game out of our half of the field. On one occasion when we managed to reach halfway, we were awarded a penalty. Andy Irvine kicked the goal, a magnificent effort.

The Springboks reacted vehemently and received their only points of this half as a result, a drop goal by Snyman. But we struck a severe and telling blow to their desperate hopes when, just on half time, we drove deep into their half, thanks to a super break by Ian McGeechan, and forced a line-out barely two yards from their goal line. As the Springboks winger Muller was retrieving the ball from the crowd, I sneaked up to the very front of the line-out as surreptitiously as possible. Muller scurried back and quickly glanced to his scrum half for the code for the throw. I crouched low, hoping that in the general hubbub and rush he would not register my positioning. He didn't. He threw the ball in for de Bruyn at number two. I jumped, caught it, and dived over the line for a try. I received a boot in the face in the process from the South African scrum half Sonnekus, which gave me an enormous black eye. As I made my way back from the goal line to our half, I felt ten feet tall.

Willie John's half-time talk was a joy. He extolled our efforts and restraints and laid it on the line what he expected from each and every one of us during the remaining forty minutes. We knew that we had the beating of them.

103

We had the breeze and the sun at our backs. Our scrum-maging was rock solid. Our line-out play was dominant. If we played with concentration, control and commitment, we could not lose. Van Heerden was singled out for having been such a troublemaker, and we agreed that he would not be allowed the same freedom in the second half.

The game restarted, and it had not been going too long when Bobby Windsor tackled Sonnekus, who had called for a mark. Despite Bobby's tackle being fair, he was immediately punched in the face by Van Heerden. I was the nearest to Bobby and immediately flew into action. Unfortunately, I had to travel about a dozen yards to get to Van Heerden and he tried to duck out of sight behind some team mates. I lunged over them, smacked him in the jaw and was immediately set upon by the whole Springboks pack. With Willie John leading the way, my team mates charged to my assistance and there commenced one of the ugliest and longest brawls ever seen on a rugby field. In the middle of it all I was punched in the face by Johann Kritzinger, the Springboks number eight. The force of the blow lifted me right off my feet and I landed flat on my back, dazed but unhurt. Amazingly my teeth were still intact. Once the whole disgraceful scene had stopped, we settled down to play some of the finest attacking rugby of the tour, culminating in two tries for J. J. Williams, following some magnificent handling of the ball by our backs.

Van Heerden still had one more defiant act of stupidity to produce. From the kick-off following J.J.'s first try he battered into Willie John with both knees dangerously raised. This was not a clever move. He was put through the mincer by the whole pack and left in a crumpled heap as the play moved away to the other side of the pitch. The game was held up for a few minutes while Van Heerden received the magic-sponge treatment from the Springboks' physio. Imagine our thoughts when we saw him shrug off the attentions of the physio, walk off the pitch and set off on the long trek up the tunnel to the dressing rooms. He was throwing in the towel! The forlorn looks on the faces of the team mates he had deserted told a lovely story if you happened to be on the other side!

The final fifteen minutes of that Test were the most enjoyable and sweetest of my rugby career. I knew that the match was won, and therefore the Test series too, and I could actually savour those thoughts while still playing. Normally the full appreciation of any success comes some hours after the event is over.

When the final whistle blew giving us victory by 26 points to 9, Bobby and I quickly hoisted Willie John onto our shoulders. I was happy, deliriously happy, at our victory and I can remember thinking, I know how I feel about it; what must *he* feel about it? We carried him to the touch-line where the whole team enjoyed the acclaim accorded us by the crowd. As Willie John was about to lead us up the tunnel to the dressing room, I quietly caught his sleeve and said, 'Willie – the boys.' I pointed up to our fellow tour-party members in the main stand who had been unsuccessful in gaining a place in the Test team but all of whom had dedicated themselves unselfishly to the cause – victory over the Springboks. We stood and saluted each other with arms raised to the blue skies. We, the team; they, our team mates. It was a very emotional experience which I will savour for ever. I wept quite openly and, despite the distance between the two groups, we were as one. We had done it.

The only black mark for me was that I had broken my hand on Van Heerden's jaw. It served me right, I suppose. It was a pity, though, because it cost me any further part in the tour. My hand was so badly swollen and sore during the last quarter of the match that I was unable to bind properly in the scrums. However Willie's normal vice-like grip on me nullified any problem I had, so the scrum remained as locked and solid as ever.

7

The Kings and I

Within the space of three years, I had played in two winning Lions series, one in New Zealand and the other in South Africa. Six of us shared in that experience, which was unique for British rugby, and although as a forward I was naturally concerned with my job and the pack in which I was working, I would like to pay tribute to our scrum half, Gareth Edwards, who was in the driving seat of the chariot, as it were, whipping and coaxing and cajoling the donkeys in front of him.

Gareth is the greatest scrum half I have ever seen. He was a superb athlete with magnificent footballing skills, all of which he demonstrated regularly on the rugby field. His performances for Wales and the Lions were gems, but his consistency over the years must be applauded too. He played superbly for the Lions in New Zealand in 1971 but for me he hit his peak in South Africa in 1974. He did not just go through the motions behind a rampant pack of forwards – he dominated us! He coaxed us to greater effort, he inspired us with his play, we all wanted to win ball for him and he rarely misused it. In the mud and glaur of the first Test at Cape Town he was a giant. On the high veldt of the Transvaal he was sheer magic: throwing out massive passes to Phil Bennett, breaking into the heart of the opponents' defence and kicking long, raking grubbers to keep us going forward. All of this rewarded our efforts in the pack.

Stories about Gareth are legion. In 1972 at Cardiff,

Scotland were leading Wales by a couple of points and we were very much in the driving seat when a sudden flash of the G. O. Edwards's brilliance changed all that. He broke round the aftermath of a line-out inside his own half and sprinted clear away deep into our territory. He kicked over the head of our fullback Arthur Brown's head, and in a thrilling hack and chase to our tryline, he controlled the ball cleverly and sustained his pace to dive on the ball to score. It was a try that broke our hearts and Wales ran away with the game thereafter. Gareth's momentum in scoring had taken him over the touch-in-goal area into the red cinder running track and his face was covered in red ash as he walked back from scoring. He wore the red ash like a proud trophy and the crowd nearly burst the stadium with their rejoicing.

He once smashed me on the nose with a tremendous punch! It was at Murrayfield and he had been stamped on by one of my team mates (Duncan Madsen, our hooker, later claimed responsibility). He was jumping about like a dervish screaming oaths galore in Scotland's direction. I was getting up from the ruck and was on one knee when he thumped me. He ran off down the pitch to follow the play, with me after him shouting, 'What the hell was that for? You little bugger.' My nose was very sore, incidentally! Mervyn Davies grabbed me, fearing I was going to administer retribution, but he immediately realized by the look on my face that that was the furthest thing from my mind. I gruffly shouted to Gareth to keep out of my way for the remainder of the game but he knew I was only bluffing. He apologized for the punch after the game and we both had a good laugh about it. 'Well, Broonie,' he said to me with a glint in his eye. 'That'll make up for all the times I wanted to punch you on tours for keeping me awake with your bloody awful snoring.'

I would also like to pay tribute to Syd Millar, our coach. He was not quite as strict as Carwyn, but he nevertheless received a superb response from the team. He also stuck to the basics, especially the scrummage, and at all times encouraged individual flair. He invited players to talk to him as much as possible about playing, training and tactics. I found him much more approachable than Carwyn, but then Syd was a forward and I was not on my first tour. All of our sessions in South Africa were relevant and varied. Blessedly, they were nearly all carried out in sunshine too. Syd tuned me to a level of fitness I had never known before and my eight tries reflected that.

He had come in for a fair bit of criticism from the press before we left Britain. Many felt that he was not up to being at the helm of a Lions tour. They were wrong. He had toured South Africa before with the Lions and his experience proved invaluable. He introduced us, verbally and physically, to the way the game is played there. 'Scrum. Scrum. Scrum,' he would say to us. 'And then we'll do some more scrumming,' he would add with a devilish chuckle.

I do not know how many scrums we did during the lead-up to the first Test – it must have been in the high hundreds – but it was our vastly superior scrummaging in poor conditions that laid the foundations for our victory in that Test and, subsequently, in the series.

Throughout the tour he demonstrated to us a phenomenal determination to wipe the floor with the Springboks. His enthusiasm for the cause was such that it was impossible not to respond to him. When it came to psychology, Syd was not as subtle as Carwyn, but he did play one masterstroke just before the second Test when the pressure was getting at us and we were showing signs of strain.

On the Friday after training was completed, Syd announced 'The Test side will all be going on a bus trip this afternoon. Report at 2.30 p.m. in the hotel foyer.' We were amazed. A bus trip? Who wanted to go on a tiring bus trip on a beautiful sunny afternoon the day before a Test match? Obedient as ever, the fifteen of us duly reported at the appointed time and off we went. Our inquiries as to where we were going and how long we were going away for received the same reply from Syd. 'Just wait and see.'

The journey lasted barely half an hour. Our destination was the summit of a hill high above Pretoria where the air was crisp and fresh, the sun was shining brightly and the birds were soaring above us in full song. We sat about on the grass for almost three hours and listened to Syd and Willie John recount stories of past tours, matches, players and incidents. The patter and humour of these two well-travelled warriors was fascinating, and it was good for our nerves to see just how relaxed and happy with life they were. My only regret about the whole afternoon was that I had not taken my tape recorder with me to record for posterity enough material to write umpteen books and speak at every rugby club dinner on the calendar for the next decade!

Willie John McBride is a man's man. He is one of the most respected forwards in the world and that is not just because the world has probably seen more of him than of anyone else. I must admit that I held him in awe, such was his reputation as an outstanding player, and my opinions did not alter after two defeats in successive seasons from Ireland in my first two years in the Scottish team.

Despite having played against him on these two occasions, I had never really been in his company until we assembled in London before the 1971 Lions tour to New Zealand. I was to room with the great man over the weekend and I felt very much the young apprentice with the mature craftsman (this was his fourth Lions tour). When he walked into the room for the first time he did not say too much, but sat down on his bed puffing away at his pipe. I was fidgeting about with my bags, trying to find some space for my blazers and flannels, etc., when Willie John asked me quietly, 'Tell me, Brownie, are you contemplating being away for an awful long time?' I looked at him inquisitively but did not know what to say. 'It's just that you've a hell of a lot of stuff there with you,' he said, putting me out of my misery. He slowly rose from his bed and still quietly puffing away at his pipe, came over to my bags. 'Now, let's just see what you've got here,' he said. He spent the next ten minutes going through all my bags, ignoring me, and dividing the contents into one small pile and one large pile. When he was finished, he pointed to the large pile and, still puffing his pipe, said, 'That lot you can post home.' I did as I was told and he was dead right!

I was impressed by him on that tour to New Zealand, but his peak came three years later when, as captain, he blazed a trail of glory in South Africa. He played the greatest rugby of his career but his leadership outshone even that!

I shall never forget how elated he was after our first Test victory in New Zealand in 1971 but that paled compared with the look on his face at the end of the third Test in South Africa. He was able to appreciate, much more than the rest of us, what that victory meant to British rugby.

To think that some of the British pressmen had doubted Willie John's fitness and ability before the tour. He dispelled those doubts with magnificent form as early as the third game. It was against Boland in Cape Province. The heat was unbearable and we really had to delve into our reserves of strength, fitness and guts. Late in the game, I fielded a high clearing kick forty yards out near touch and set off for the line. I managed to raise quite a head of steam and charged through some tacklers before finally being sunk, agonizingly, four yards short. But guess who was at my elbow to take a pop-up pass and romp home for his only try of the tour? Willie John. Not bad for a guy supposed to be 'Dad's Army' material. And in that searing heat.

The result of the second Test – and the third, for that matter – belied the effort and the fire that the Springbok forwards put into each game. We played fifteen-man attacking rugby in those two Tests off a very strong forward base. In New Zealand in 1971, despite the magnificent running and counterattacking of our backs, we nevertheless generally played ten-man rugby during the

Test matches; in South Africa in 1974 it was almost the opposite case and yet the South African tour has never been acknowledged as being a great running series. Some critics reckoned that we should have scored double the number of points in the second and third Tests, but it was not as easy as that. The Springbok selectors certainly assisted our efforts by chopping and changing their team quite regularly. We on the other hand used no more than seventeen players throughout the four Tests.

When looking at all the players that we played against during my three Lions tours I think that the 1971 All Blacks pack that played in the first Test, with the back division that we played against in New Zealand in 1977 in the third Test, would be extremely difficult to beat. The team which I reckon would maybe just do that job would be a combination of the pack from the 1974 and 1977 Lions tours with the back division from the 1971 Lions tour. What a game that would be!

My top Lions team, chosen from all the players I have played alongside, would be:

J. P. R. Williams (J.P.R.)
Gerald Davies (Reames)
John Dawes (captain) (Sid)
Mike Gibson (Gibbo)
David Duckham (Duckers)
Barry John (King)
Gareth Edwards (Gar or Pinocchio)
Ian McLauchlan (Mighty Mouse)
Peter Wheeler (Wheelbrace)
Fran Cotton (Frannie)
Bill Beaumont (Billy the Bum, or Reg)
G. L. Brown (Broon, or Stoochie)
Tony Neary (Nero)
Mervyn Davies (Swerve)
Fergus Slattery (Slatts)

My choice, I know, will surprise the fraternity of prop forwards. They say that for pure strength, and even purer technique, Ray McLoughlin, of Ireland, was without peer in the modern game, either as a tight-head or as a loose-head. Some say that Ray would have eaten Fran Cotton and Ian McLauchlan on either side of the scrum in the same afternoon. All I know is that I found Ray difficult to scrummage behind.

Admittedly, I only played behind him once in 1971, in the first game in New Zealand against Thames Valley and Counties at Pukekohe, because at that stage of the tour I was mostly in the second team. Ray had broken his thumb on Alex Wyllie's jaw in the Canterbury game and had gone home before I got into the Test team. Still, I have to say that I found it uncomfortable to scrummage behind him because he scrummaged so low and at such an awkward angle. John Pullin, our hooker, said much the same thing to Ray and that he would prefer to scrummage a bit higher. 'Well, you'll just have to get used to it,' said Ray. Nobody was inclined to argue with a technician of Ray's calibre.

Ray McLoughlin's generation of props were destroyers rather than generators of shove. They were concerned with making their immediate opponent so uncomfortable that the whole of the opposing scrum disintegrated. In the early part of the 1970s, the trend was towards eight-man shoves, and therefore a prop's value, at least to his locks, was in the way he was able to transmit shove coming through from behind.

Maybe this happened because the ability of hookers as strikers was in such sharp decline. I know that present-day hookers are regarded as a joke by the artists of ten and fifteen years ago. 'All they do is stick a leg out on their own ball,' say the old timers, 'and push on the other side's ball. Half the time their own ball is not even contested by the opposing hooker, so they don't have to be any good at all. Anyone can play international rugby as a hooker these days.' There is some truth in that, but although it may be regarded as heresy to say so, I would still rather scrum-mage behind Ian McLauchlan or Fran Cotton than Ray McLoughlin.

Fran Cotton could have propped up London's Tower Bridge. His strength and technique at scrummaging were so sound that he played loose-head and tight-head at Test level with equal success. He stood no nonsense from anyone. At the 'awkward time' on match days between lunch and actually leaving the hotel for the stadium, Fran and I had a ritual of listening to my cassette thumping out Rolling Stones music at top volume. It seemed to have a soothing effect on our minds while stimulating the flow of adrenaline in our bodies.

Another of my choices which might raise a few eye-brows is that of Tony Neary. After all, he only played in one Test on two tours, and in choosing him and Fergus Slattery, I have opted for two flankers who are basically open-sides. Ignoring the sniffs from those who say my chances in the line-out would be lessened with either Slatts or Nero behind me, I must point out that when Tony Neary was called in to lead the forwards against Auckland and in the final Test against New Zealand in 1977, he excelled himself and received a full response from the whole pack. I rated him so highly that I was delighted when England dropped him from their team to play Scotland! His mobil-ity about the field was a great asset, and he always made his presence felt at breakdown situations.

I am sure that no one would argue about Mervyn Davies. I never really saw Ken Goodall, but in my time Mervyn was the best number eight in the world. He scrummaged with purpose, his line-out play was dex-trous, his defence was superb and his mobility was never questioned. It was only when he ceased playing that the Welsh fully appreciated his ability and worth. He has never been replaced. His performances in South Africa with the Lions in 1974 were quite magnificent.

Fergus Slattery is the nearest thing I have seen to a human flying-machine. He put more pressure on stand-off

113

halves round the world than any other wing forward I have seen. He regularly pushed himself brutally beyond the limit at training sessions in order to maintain his razor sharpness on the field. He had a zest for life that at times bordered on the insane, and his emotional rendering of Irish rebel songs never failed to arouse the team's feelings and get the blood pumping, no matter the circumstances.

What a player, what a character, what a tourist Peter Wheeler is. He can hook, he is hard, he can play in the loose and he can throw in. Indeed, he is the finest thrower-in of the ball I have ever played with. This helped me enormously against Andy Haden in New Zealand in 1977. Peter is a great realist and humorist, and he contributed a great deal to the annihilation of the New Zealand packs in 1977.

8

A Sporting Pedigree

And to think that I could have been an everyday soccer player all my life! Perhaps I would have been, too, if it had not been for one incident during a soccer match at Troon in 1964 when I was only sixteen years old. I was the goalkeeper for Troon Juniors during a West of Scotland cup tie against Irvine Meadow, then the premier junior side in Scotland. Five hundred or so spectators were crowded into Portland Park, Troon, which is a neat, well-grassed and generally well-looked after ground, and the score, going into the second half, was 1 goal each. In no time, however, the Meadow's right winger, 'Hooky' Walker, began to cut loose and run rings round my defenders like a Tom Finney possessed. Now Hooky was in the twilight of what had been a very successful career in junior football and was, of course, the darling of the Meadow crowd – and the whole of Irvine for that matter! The Meadow supporters and his team mates warmed to his efforts that afternoon. He set up chance after chance for his fellow forwards and in no time the inevitable happened – goals two, three, four, five and six were duly stuck into the back of the net behind me! Only one of them I could possibly have saved. The rest gave me no chance. With two minutes remaining and me absolutely shattered, Hooky broke clean through the defence on his own with only me to beat. As his supporters' chants of 'Hooky! Hooky!' rang in my ears, he steadied himself to score the goal which he thoroughly deserved and which would send his faithful home happy. But it was not to be. I unceremoniously upended him at the edge of the penalty box as he tried to run round me to score. The crowd were incensed and went berserk. Pennies and halfpennies (the pre-decimal and, therefore, larger and heavier versions) rained down on my head from everywhere. I was terrified! The resultant penalty kick could not be taken, because I could not stand in the goal mouth.

Eventually I was saved from the mob by two local policemen, Inspector Stephen and Sergeant Elder. They were both regular spectators at Troon Junior matches over the years but probably neither of them had ever been involved professionally at a match before.

The Irvine captain showed not the slightest thought of my wellbeing in nominating the left half, a huge, rugged man with bright red hair, to take the spot kick. Why had he not selected Hooky to take it? I would have thankfully dived out of the way of the ball to ensure a goal and, therefore, appease the spectators, who, despite the presence of the 'polis', were still, after all, only two yards away behind my goal. I could hear their breath and I could read their lips – and that was with my back to them!

The penalty kick was duly smashed home and the referee immediately blew his whistle for time. I did not retrieve the ball from the back of the net. For all I cared, it could stay there for ever. All I wanted to do was exit. The polis duly escorted me across to the dressing-room door and as I entered I heard a voice with a distinct Irvine twang to it say, 'We'll come back and get the bugger when he comes out in half an hour!' Well, I was out in two minutes and, still in my football gear with my clothes tucked under my arm, I ran out of the ground as fast as I could and never stopped till safely home in Academy Street, half a mile away.

I never went back to Portland Park. Two days later I reported to Marr College FP Rugby Club for training. My serious rugby career was born.

It was in this way that I turned my back on the chance of following in my father's footsteps into the soccer hall of fame. He had played professionally as goalkeeper for Clyde, Hibs, Dundee and Kilmarnock, winning the Scottish Cup with Clyde in 1938, and had been capped for Scotland. In his teens, he had served his apprenticeship as a player in amateur and junior football in Ayrshire. During one lean spell, he even started up his own team in Troon, personally raising the funds for all the strips, kit and equipment.

One of his greatest claims to fame was that during the cup-winning campaign in 1938 with Clyde he only conceded one goal and that was a penalty kick in the semifinal against Rangers. Recently the story was romantically retold to me by a very elderly gent in a Glasgow public house. He was a Clyde supporter – still loyal, too – and with quivering voice he proudly told me of his devotion to Clyde and his admiration for my father as a goalkeeper. He took me through the cup blow by blow and when he spoke of the one goal that Dad let in the veins on his forehead stood out like horns, his face became red and puffy, and he roared, 'And it wisnae a bloody penalty!' What beautiful, lingering emotion – even if unabashedly biased.

My father was one of the first goalkeepers to advance from his goal line to meet an oncoming player in order to narrow the shooting angle – a commonplace reaction from all goalkeepers nowadays. He saved many situations which others would have lost, but of course sometimes the tactic backfired, leaving him stranded and the goal wide open. He also had a penchant for saving penalty kicks, studying the different techniques of all the known penalty-takers of each team so that he always knew which corner of the net they favoured.

His first full-time wage with Clyde was £4 per week – quite different from the massive sums now awarded to top players. The early-season training which 'Matha' Gemmill put the Clyde players through was 'every bit as murderous as any rugby sessions I've seen nowadays'. My father points out that the sharpness required by all soccer

117

players compares with that of rugby backs, but he adds that forwards in rugby require a completely different type of fitness, including stamina, strength, 'and stacks of courage!'

In those days the football season finished at the end of April and did not recommence until 12 August – the 'Glorious Twelfth' had a different meaning for some folk! Almost three and a half months' break between seasons is a far cry from today's demands.

Two of my father's brothers were also senior soccer players. Tom played as goalie for Ipswich Town and James as centre forward for Manchester United. James first found fame in America with the New York Giants and played for America in their World Cup campaign in Uruguay in 1930 when they reached the semifinals! They were defeated 7–1 by Argentina in a bruising, dirty game in which the Argentinians were very much the aggressors. The game was actually a replay even although the American team *won* the first quite sporting game by 2–1. Ten minutes after full time, however, the referee had walked into their dressing room and advised them that he'd chalked off their second goal! Hence the replay.

When James was travelling by boat from America to sign for Manchester United manager Scott Duncan, he was 'intercepted' by the Hearts manager, Willie McCartney, as the boat lay off the 'tail of the bank' awaiting high tide before docking at Greenock. McCartney hired a tug to take him out to the ocean-going liner but his desperate efforts were in vain because of the deal already struck between the boss of New York Giants and Scott Duncan. At that time my father was playing for Hibs in Edinburgh, along with Matt Busby, later to take over as manager at Manchester United from Scott Duncan.

My father gained his first cap against Wales alongside another famous manager-to-be, also gaining his first cap that day, Bill Shankly. Dad finished his playing career at Kilmarnock and, being a qualified physiotherapist, took up the post of trainer at Killie. He also at that time started to develop his own private practice in Troon.

I loved going to the football with him, whether it was a training day or a match day. I can remember one day wandering away from Rugby Park (believe it or not, that is the name of Kilmarnock's ground) while Dad was training the players. It was just before my fourth birthday and I eventually found myself at the Cross, right in the heart of town. I had crossed four main roads on the way and God knows how I was not killed. Eventually I burst into tears and told a lady that I was lost. She led me to a policewoman and in no time at all I was inside the police station telling the duty sergeant that my father was Mr Brown and I had lost him at the football. An hour later one very worried father entered to report his son missing, only to be met with the sight of yours truly sitting on top of the police counter singing 'A Gordon for Me' to all and sundry. On realizing the situation, the duty sergeant boomed out to my father, 'For goodness' sake, tell you son his father is not Mr Brown – but Big Jock Broon!' I never got lost again.

Good enough to become a scratch golfer, my father played in the British Open championship when it came to Troon in 1962. He did not, however, threaten Arnold Palmer's dominance! What a pity the deftness of his hands – so obvious at soccer, golf, badminton and physiotherapy – was never given the chance to be displayed on a rugby field. He never played once!

He became the physiotherapist to Scotland's rugby team in 1969 after Jim Telfer, then Scotland's skipper, complained because he had been made available to the Springboks but not to us! He had previously, voluntarily, helped the Australians and the All Blacks during their tours, especially when they had stayed in Troon prior to playing in Glasgow. He was with the All Blacks at Murrayfield when Colin Meads was sent off. He loved every minute of the time he was with the Scottish team and I can unbiasedly say the feelings were mutual. His room at the hotel always became the team focal point, whether for

119

treatment, chat, fruit, sweets or literature!

I will never forget Dad coming onto the pitch at Murrayfield, during a game against England, to attend my brother Peter who had received a thump on the head. The magic sponge was not getting much response from Peter and I was beginning to fear he might have to go off, when Dad asked him, 'When's Margaret's [my mother's] birthday?' I thought he'd say, 'Who's Margaret?' such was his state. When he replied 'A week on Tuesday,' we knew he was OK.

Dad retired from the rugby scene, rather prematurely according to most, following Scotland's victory in Dublin in 1976. It was fate that he made his mind up to stop when he did because if he had stayed on he would have been in an embarrassing situation the following season with my sending-off and suspension.

My mother was the penalty queen of the hockey team. As centre forward she scored many cracking goals but as a penalty-taker she was dead-eyed. She never missed! Mum also performed well at netball, proving that the ball-playing ability and coordination which my brothers and I thankfully possess have been passed to us from both parents. I hope the sporting family tree continues with my daughter, Mardi, and son Rory. There certainly is nothing lacking in their pedigree!

Next to the main rugby pitch at Marr was the hockey pitch and often during a lull in play I used to look across to watch a lovely, young redhead, her long hair tied up in bunches with matching ribbons, running about on her toes, whacking the hockey ball with amazing power. Her name was Linda Hastings and she was to become my wife. Many a Saturday night we both used to limp into the cinema complaining to each other of bruised shins and ankles.

Linda was a dab hand at hockey, golf and swimming. She came from a very famous golfing family. Her father Willie Hastings had been a golf professional for over thirty years at Kilmarnock Barassie Club and had won the

Scottish PGA championship; her sister Joan had been the Scottish Ladies' champion and a member of the British Ladies' Curtis Cup team. Her mother Betty regularly picks up trophies at the annual prize-giving of the Troon Bentinck Ladies' Golf Club.

My brother Peter has saved my life fifty times. That's just about how many times my brother John was going to murder me had Peter not come to my rescue. John and I fought constantly. We could not pass each other in a room without niggling at one another. I am relieved to report that the older we both got, the better things were between us and the safer my life became!

John enjoyed his rugby at school but left before he had the chance to play in the first XV. On leaving school he chose golf as his main pastime and ended up with a handicap of four at Troon Portland Golf Club. Only when he reached his late twenties did he start playing rugby again, at Marr, where as a lock he helped them win the fourth-division championship one season. On the few occasions I saw John play, I was amazed at the natural ball sense and playing ability he displayed. He never achieved any great level of fitness but was nevertheless regularly to the fore in all matches. I honestly believe that had he kept on playing rugby when he left school, he would have undoubtedly gone the whole way to international level. Peter, John and I only ever played together once – just before I retired, in an invitation game fittingly enough at Marr.

We do play more regularly together at golf and father Brown makes up the four. We three are always wanting to partner 'the old man' because he's by far the most reliable player of us all. We once all went to see Scotland versus England at Hampden Park, Glasgow. The stadium was packed and there was no room to be had anywhere. Except behind us! Father 6 feet 2 inches, Peter 6 feet 3 inches, John 6 feet 4½ inches, and me 6 feet 5 inches. Would you stand behind us?

121

9

The Man on the Coathanger

I loved football. Inter-class matches at school were played for a whole week, each game commencing on Monday morning and progressing at intervals throughout the week until the bell ending the Friday mid-afternoon break. The scores were sometimes in the hundreds but we never lost count!

Within minutes of the school bus dropping me at home each afternoon, I was into my football gear, hurrying down to the Darley golf course to meet my pals Davie Ritson, Jimmy Robertson, Frank Powell and many more for shooting-in, dribbling or full-blooded matches. We used a corner of the golf course, nicknamed the 'Wee Patch', and lived our fantasy worlds galore.

Sometimes my brother Peter, six years my elder, would play at shooting-in with me out in 'the Park', the name affectionately given to a large and very uneven piece of waste ground situated behind our house. I loved it when Peter spent time with me. He showed me how to kick the ball harder, volley on the turn, curve the ball with my instep and swerve it with the outside of my foot. He coached me on goalkeeping, enhancing my ability to time my jumps to the high ball and my dives to the low ones. He taught me to keep my eye on the ball at all times – one of my father's greatest tips, too. In years to come Peter and I were to spend many hours together practising kicking and catching, but this time with a ball of a different shape.

At the age of ten, I took a leaf out of my father's book

and with my pals started up our own football team, Muirhead Rovers. We played our challenge matches against sides which were in general older than ourselves, and although not always victorious we always gave a good account of ourselves. Polo Corinthians, Gillies Street Rangers, Andy Thom's Mob and the Barassie Boys all provided great opposition and many memories. At that time I played anywhere in the team, but my favourite positions were centre forward and goalkeeper.

My final year at primary school saw me play in my first rugby match. The game was against Dalry Primary School at Dalry. I was eleven years old. The PE teacher was Jack Morrison, whom I was to meet again in later years in New Zealand and whose protégé there almost put me out of the Lions tour. He gave us our dark green jerseys on the Friday and I will never forget modelling mine with pride when I got home. I could have taken on the world! I dreamed that night that I had scored ten tries and converted them all. In reality, playing stand-off I scored the only try of the match.

At Marr College, Troon's senior secondary school, I came under the guidance of a fanatical, rugby-loving PE teacher, Keir 'Papa' Hardie. Rugby was virtually compulsory at Marr as no other sports were available, at that time, to boys. The very first day Papa Hardie clapped eyes on me he bellowed in a very crisp, well-spoken accent, 'Well, boy, you've a lot to live up to you know. Your brother Peter [who had just left Marr] was one of the best rugby players I've ever had at this school. If you can emulate him you'll be doing damned well!' This did not demoralize me one bit. Instead I felt great pride at what he had said about Peter and a fierce determination welled up inside me. I was determined to emulate him.

After only ten minutes of the very first rugby practice I was moved by Papa from stand-off to second row and apart from the odd sojourn at number eight, there I was to stay to the day I retired. I was appointed captain of the first-year first XV.

123

We were undefeated that year, thanks largely to my second-row partner, Tommy 'Big Nellie' Nelson, who was slightly older than the rest of us and far and away the biggest in our team. He used to run in the tries from way out. Our arch rivals were Ayr Academy. If we beat every other team but lost to Ayr, the season was a disaster; conversely, if we lost to everyone else but beat Ayr, the season was a success. It is virtually the same feeling, for better or worse, which many Scots have about our national XV against England.

The constant comparisons between me and Peter by all and sundry, and especially by Papa Hardie, continued to stimulate me. I had this feeling that no matter where I was playing I was always being watched, and I responded to that pressure. Peter was now an international rugby player. How proud I was going to Murrayfield on the school bus to see my big brother playing for Scotland against France. Scotland won, too! Yet all of that might never have been: I remember Peter nearly bleeding to death after kneeling on a broken bottle in Fullarton Woods, Troon. He severed an artery and the blood was gushing from the wound. Luckily one of our friends knew how to apply a tourniquet and, with the excellent aid of a nearby householder, Peter's life was saved.

During my third year I once missed the school bus for an away game against Glasgow Academy and had to play for the second XV against Ardrossan Academy. I scored five tries and converted the lot in our 25–0 defeat of Ardrossan. I was tempted to miss the bus again but I am sure that no one would have believed that it was an accident. I was on a real high at that time, having just won the Troon junior badminton championship gent's doubles with Keith Martin and the mixed doubles with Sandra Nicol.

Of the rugby moments of my third year, I will never forget scoring the only drop goal of my *whole* rugby career and also converting a try with my left foot, both at the college ground in Troon. *The* highlight was playing in the school first XV at the end of the season to become only the fourth player in the school's history to do so whilst still in the third year. Guess who one of the others was? Yes, Peter! I played in the first XV for the whole of the next year and relished every minute of it. I was invited to play in the senior Ayrshire school trial but was ignored and progressed no further.

I mixed rugby and soccer quite seriously during my fourth year at school. I played rugby on Saturday mornings for Marr and soccer in the afternoons, first for Ayr Albion (under-sixteens), with whom I won league- and cup-winners' medals, and then Troon Waverley, a team full of men.

When I left school at the end of my fourth year I joined the British Linen Bank in Ayr. I had to work every Saturday morning, which forced me to make the choice of rugby or soccer as my main sport. My father did not try to influence my decision in any way. All he said was, 'Play the sport you think you'll enjoy most.' Whilst deliberating, I recommenced playing goalie for Troon Juniors and, at the same time, trained for the coming rugby season with Marr College FP. Then along came a West of Scotland cup tie at Portland Park, Troon, against Irvine Meadow, who had a right winger named Hooky Walker . . .

The longer I was with Marr FP the more my brother Peter influenced me. The constant comparisons drawn between Peter and me by team mates, the opposition and the press only seemed an encouragement to strive harder. Being Peter's wee brother was hard to live up to but it was never a drawback! He was always advising and encouraging me and showing me his techniques, and although I never became a duplicate of him – that would not be possible anyway, because Peter's ways were unique – I learned much that was helpful to me. Having moved from Muirhead to live only two hundred yards from the water's edge, we used to spend hours on Troon beach, kicking a rugby ball back and forth to each other. Sometimes we did it in our bare feet. I became quite adept at punting and

place-kicking with both feet; my fielding of the high ball –
especially with the sea breezes blowing it all over the place
– became second nature. We practised mauling and close-
quarter tackling in a confined space, which was of great
value to me because Peter was then so much heavier than I
was. We used to have some great line-out battles when we
had Peter's fiancée (now wife) Jill to throw the ball in for
us. I suspected Jill used to favour my side a wee bit just to
make Peter work that much harder.

The cottage we had moved to in Academy Street had a
hatch into the loft in the ceiling of the hallway. Peter was
very adept at springing to catch the ridge of the hatch; he
was able to do it time and again with enviable dexterity.
Even although I was by now at least an inch taller than
him, it took me hours of practising and a few bleeding
fingers but, joy of joys, I eventually managed it. There was
no holding me back thereafter and another gap between
the two of us had closed.

Peter and I had a perpetual challenge about heading
the ball during matches. We used to pay each other
sixpence each time either of us did it. Needless to say he
won more money than I – but then heading the ball was
one of Peter's many trademarks. One of my headers
actually led to Marr winning a game against Stirling
County at Stirling. We were drawing 3–3 with only
seconds left to play and Stirling had a drop-out 25. I called
for the ball, but it hung in the air a fraction longer than I
anticipated and I could sense that Stirling forwards were
timing their run-up to me to perfection. I was going to be
minced! Instead of catching the ball I headed it over them,
still keeping it in play; at the same time I was clattered into
the mud! The referee blew for a penalty to Marr because I
had been tackled without the ball and Bob Yates, our
gifted stand-off, duly converted the kick to make the final
score 6–3 in our favour. The Stirling County boys were
not happy!

During my second season with Marr FP I was selected
to play for Ayrshire against Renfrewshire – my first

representative match. It was played at Whitecraigs one cold, damp, grey evening. The standard of rugby was hardly scintillating on the muddy and uneven pitch, but I nevertheless had a good game. After the match a combined team was to be selected to play against the senior Glasgow team the following week. The Marr supporters present were already in the bar celebrating what was for them a foregone conclusion – my selection! I was quietly sitting with an orange juice, just keeping my fingers crossed and hoping to be given my first real crack at the man who meant most – Peter! Alas, the selectors looked beyond the teams of that evening and brought in John McHarg, a stalwart then of Irvine Rugby Club, where he played second row with his young brother Alistair. I was very disappointed of course and more than a bit embarrassed at the hullabaloo the Marr supporters kicked up. I was absolutely blazing when I later heard that the main reason I had been left out was because the selectors reckoned that Peter and I would just have a carry-on against each other and not take it very seriously.

The following season I *was* selected for the combined XV to play against Glasgow and I am the proud owner of newspaper cuttings which highlight my victory over Peter in the line-outs. Team talks and tactics were wasted on me that night. I already had my goal! I felt the same way whenever I played against Peter.

The end of Saturday-morning working at the bank left me free finally to follow Peter's footsteps and join his club, West of Scotland, one of the top senior sides in Scotland. It was a move I had longed for and one I never regretted. I had been up at West with Peter on quite a few occasions and so knew most of the players already, and I held most of them in awe! I had even travelled in the West team bus to some matches whilst I had been injured and unable to play for Marr.

One dream that was not to be fulfilled at this stage was playing alongside Peter. He moved to the Borders before the new season started to take up an appointment with a

firm of chartered accountants in Galashiels and joined
Gala. Sadly, I missed the Gala versus West encounter that
season because I was recuperating from a cartilage operation.

With Peter unavailable for Scotland's tour of the
Argentine, it was the following season before I finally
played in the same team as him. We were selected as
second-row partners in a Scottish XV to play the Combined Services at Murrayfield. I was really excited at the
prospect and felt very proud. The irony was that we were
vying with each other for the selectors' nod to partner
Peter Stagg in the Scotland team ten days later to play
against the Springboks at Murrayfield. This fact was even
mentioned to us by Jim Telfer in his prematch team talk.
Needless to say, at every line-out during the game Jim
Telfer had to put up with Peter and me both shouting to
him, 'My ball!'

Imagine my feelings when, after that game, it was my
name and not Peter's which was included in the Scotland
team to play the South Africans. After all the years of
living in Peter's shadow, and the constant comparisons, I
felt that I had arrived. I was still 'Peter Brown's wee
brother' – but I was now upsides with him!

I had arrived home to be given an even more exuberant
than normal welcome from the family pet mongrel dog,
Mhuilach. I tried to calm him down as I entered the living
room where my parents were sitting. 'What on earth is
pleasing him so much?' I asked.

My mother replied, 'Maybe he's heard that you've been
capped to play for Scotland against the Springboks this
Saturday.'

I could not believe it. 'What about Peter?' I asked.

'No Peter,' was the reply. 'He's not even on the
bench.'

Once the hugging and kissing and back-slapping was
over I could not wait to tell all my pals, so I rushed off
round the town to spread the news. I could not find
anybody! I could not even phone my fiancée Linda,

ve: Absolutely drained! Showing the
n of victory at the end of the Second
t in South Africa, 1974. There's no
ion, just an immense feeling of a job
done

Below: The Third Test and the series are
in the bag! One of the most emotional
moments of my rugby career as
Willie-John and I salute our non-playing
team-mates up in the stand

Above: Scoring from a line-out for the
Lions in the Third Test in South Africa. I
receive a boot in the face too from their
scrum-half, Sonnekus

Below: 'Here, Gareth, just the way
like it.' South Africa, 1974, Third T

er Uttley and I making friends in
e Town, 1974. Isn't she a wee
sher?

With Gary Player, fresh from his
British Open victory at Royal
Birkdale, prior to our historic
game in South Africa, 1974

e undefeated Lions of 1974. *Standing, back row:* T. David, M. Burton, F. Cotton, C.
ston, R. Uttley, A. Ripley, T. Grace, A. Neary, A. Irvine. *Standing, middle row:* C.
ser, R. Milliken, S. McKinney, F. Slattery, G. Evans, R. Bergiers, G. Brown, A. Old,
Kennedy, W. Steele. *Sitting:* S. Carmichael, M. Davies, I. McLauchlan, S. Millar,
. McBride, A. Thomas, J.P.R. Williams, M. Gibson (Replacement). *Front:* J.
loney, C. Rees, R. Windsor, P. Bennett, J.J. Williams, G. Edwards, I. McGeechan

'Any tacklers?' Sandy Carmichael leading the charge for Scotland

'Mighty Mouse' and Big Al on the rampage. Need I say more?

Gareth Edwards, the greatest scrum-half in the world, making another stand-off very happy. New Zealand's Ian Kirkpatrick can do nothing about it

ry John, 'The King', slipping away
Fergus Slattery, 'The Human
amo'

One for me and the Baa-Baas from Peter
Whiting and the All Blacks, Twickenham,
1974

Prince of Wingers, David Duckham, producing his brand of royal rugby to score for
Lions against North Auckland in New Zealand, 1971

New Zealand, 1977, against Wellington. Running onto Brynmor Williams' inside pass

One of my favourite sights in rugby: watching Andy Irvine on another defence-splitting sortie. For the Lions against Taranaki in New Zealand, 1977. Graham Mourie, later to become a celebrated All Black captain, tries to head him off

n off Cape Horn! Mighty and I have
ne success off the field too in South
rica, 1974

Just what does a bored Lion get
up to during a wet and windy
afternoon in New Zealand, 1977?

nd Test, New Zealand, 1977. Terry Cobner reminds the forwards that back home
e lights are coming on in the valleys'

Young Bristol and West Building Society executive, seen here with Sandy Niven of W.D. & H.O. Wills, 1982

My big brothers, John and Peter, and I a Marr in 1979. Regrettably, the only time we ever played together

Norman Sanson — another Troonite. He went on from being my patrol leader in Troc Boy Scouts to become the world's top referee. His efforts went a long way in helping t stamp out thuggery in the game at the top-class level. Sadly, he retired prematurely, somewhat disillusioned at the lack of support he received from some unions because her flat in Edinburgh had no phone.

The press spent the next few days almost living with me. I never realized there were so many sports writers in Scotland, and they all wanted something different for their own publication. The attention I received was incredible, and I loved it!

The day after the team announcement was made a note was passed round Marr College by the Rector declaring a half-day holiday in honour of my selection. As the pupils left the school later that day a boy shouted out to all and sundry, 'Three cheers for Gordon Brown – whoever he is!'

I was as high as a kite all week long. The penny dropped when I arrived in Edinburgh on Thursday to join the rest of the team. It was a great experience simply to train with the team that day and the thought going through my head was, 'If I feel this good about training, what on earth am I going to feel like on Saturday, actually playing?'

I enjoyed every minute of the build-up to the kick-off. My nerves were being soothed throughout by a tip given by Peter when he phoned to congratulate me on my selection. 'Just think of how you'll feel running out on the pitch with the crowd roaring in your ears.' It was something which I had dreamed about for years and now it was actually going to happen – it was fantastic.

On the day, my excitement was at fever pitch. I relished the journey to the ground. The bus weaved its way through the traffic and red lights, following two motorcycle outriders who were like two Indian scouts ahead of the cavalry. I had a marvellous feeling as the bus turned into Murrayfield. I was not there just to watch as before: I was actually going to play! The dressing-room atmosphere was very emotional. When I pulled the Scotland jersey over my head I caught a glimpse of myself in the far corner mirror. I was nearly in tears and gave myself a big cheesy grin and a wink, a personal routine I was to follow every time I played at Murrayfield thereafter.

The crowd hubbub grew steadily louder as we completed our warm-up. Skipper, Jim Telfer, was going over

129

last-minute exhortations. I ignored the bit about Frik De Preez (my opposite number) being one of the greatest line-out jumpers in the world. Let him worry about me, I thought, trying hard to believe it!

'Two minutes to go,' someone called from the body of the kirk. I looked across the dressing room and spied my father. He was supposed to be physiotherapist to the Springboks, but Jim Telfer had objected to them having a physio when we did not so Dad was duly transferred. He gave me a lovely nod and smile that said more to me than all the talking during the week. 'One minute,' the faceless voice advised. Just time for me to read again the note of good wishes Linda had sent me. Of all the letters and telegrams I had received, that one meant the most.

Bang! bang! on the door. 'Let's go, lads,' and we were away down the corridor to the top of the tunnel. By this time I had an unbelievable lump in my throat and tears in my eyes. If anyone had asked me something I would have been unable to reply. We were given the come-on by the steward at the bottom of the tunnel. We started to trot. I could see the crowd away on the far side of the terracing, their Lion Rampant flags dancing and waving in the wind. I could heard the band playing 'Scotland the Brave'. The farther down the tunnel I trotted the more I thought that I would never get out of that wee hole at the bottom. I seemed to be getting bigger and bigger with every stride. In all the dreams I had had about this moment, I underestimated fifty-fold.

When the band finally left the pitch I took up position to field the kick-off. When the whistle blew and the ball flew towards me I could hardly see it because of the tears in my eyes, such was the emotion of the moment. I caught the ball and the whole Springbok pack caught me! The emotion evaporated and the game was reality.

In no time at all I was back in the dressing room hardly believing that the game was already over. It had all gone so quickly and I was feeling on top of the world because we had won by 6 points to 3. We scored the only try of the match by Ian Smith, our fullback, following a devastating break at centre by John Frame.

The champagne flowed at the North British Hotel that night and I was desperately trying to take in as much of the atmosphere, the feelings, and the events as was poss-ible because I knew that day was unique. During the match I ran faster, jumped higher, and scrummaged harder than ever before, such was the adrenaline being pumped through my body. Yet at eleven o'clock that night I felt as fresh as a daisy. Reality reasserted itself on Sunday morning when I attempted to rise from my bed – I could not move an inch! Every bone, muscle and ligament in my body was at screaming pitch as though they had been through a mangle. I very slowly struggled to a bath and after soaking in it for two hours I started to feel some little relief. It took me fully two weeks to recover physically from the match.

Despite his obvious disappointment at not being chosen Peter had been, nevertheless, genuinely delighted at my selection. He gave me many valuable hints in my build-up to the game. I retained my place for the following game against France, at Murrayfield, but our defeat then had the press calling for some changes.

I was working in the bank, patiently awaiting news of Scotland's team to go to Wales, when I was told that there was someone on the phone who had to do with rugby. I rushed to the phone and the conversation went like this.

Me: Hello?'

'Great news – I'm back in the Scottish team!' my brother yelled excitedly down the phone.

'Fantastic!' I shouted. 'Who's out?'

'You are,' he replied.

I suppose only my beloved brother could break such awful news to me in that manner. On hearing the names of the team, Mother did not know whether to laugh or cry. However, at least I was still part of the squad; I had been nominated to travel with the team as substitute.

We made a bit of history in Wales because early in the

second half Peter pulled a calf muscle badly and had to leave the pitch. I substituted for him! It was a peculiar feeling to be cold in the stand high above the field of play one minute and the next to be right in the thick of it. Someone in the Welsh pack gave me a welcoming bang in the stomach as soon as I appeared on the pitch, winding me badly, and by the time I managed to regain my wind the game was all but over. It was a hellishly frustrating experience. One wag had the audacity to suggest afterwards that if Peter and I worked it properly we ought to be able to give each other about twenty caps apiece!

Peter and I were at long last selected together to play for Scotland against England in the last match of the 1970 championship. Frank Laidlaw of Melrose was the new skipper and Tom Elliott, a great player, sadly neglected by the selectors for too long, came into the back row alongside Peter and Roger Arneil. Peter took over from Jim Telfer at number eight. Jock Turner of Gala was brought back at centre to join John Frame as the direct opposition against England's golden boys, God One and God Two – David Duckham and John Spencer respectively – who were on the crest of a wave in English jerseys.

The shackles were off that day at Murrayfield and we went on the rampage. Every one of us played right out of our skins. It was fire and fury all the way, with a spirit I had never encountered to date throughout the Scottish side. The forwards produced the possession and, with Ian Robertson at his silky best at stand-off, the backs produced the exciting thrusts and the tries – a forty-yarder from Alastair Biggar and the second from Jock Turner after a sizzling scissors with Ian Robertson. That gave us victory by 14 points to 5. Peter and I played alongside each other in the Scottish team on ten further occasions, though never once as second-row partners.

Peter loved to display to the full his magnificent ball-playing skills and was liable to be seen all over the place doing all sorts of weird and wonderful things with a rugby ball. His reverse cross-field pass had to be seen to be believed! He was labelled by some as 'too loose' a player, but although at times this accusation had some substance, it should not detract from the fact that he was an excellent scrummager, a prolific ball-winner at the line-outs and no shirker when it came to rucking and mauling.

His deflections at the line-out had a deftness to them that I have only seen from a very few, and his peculiarly angular shape could make him a most awkward opponent. Rhys Williams, the Wales and British Lions lock forward, hit the nail on the head when he once described Peter as 'the man on the coathanger'.

He captained Scotland ten times, an honour which sadly eluded me, and a damned good job he made of it! His first game as captain was against France in Paris in 1971. We were going well and had our noses in front, but one incident changed everything – Jean-Pierre Bastiat's late tackle on our fullback Ian Smith. Bastiat should have been ordered off, such was the brutality and lateness of his charge. But of course in these days a player almost had to carry out murder before ordering off could even be considered. Ian Smith was carried off and Brian Simmers, that gifted footballer from Glasgow Academicals, came on as substitute. He went to stand-off and Jock Turner moved to fullback in Smith's place. This was a prematch decision and, with Peter being so inexperienced as a captain at this level, one that was adhered to. The changes completely upset our team rhythm and hindsight told us that we probably would have won the game had Brian gone straight to fullback. Jock had been playing a blinder, being involved in everything, and his cover tackling on the intruding French fullback Pierre Villepreux was devastating. It was impossible for Brian Simmers to come on cold as substitute and pick up where Jock left off. It was Villepreux's late intrusion try which clinched the game for France by 13 points to 8.

This was my first visit to Paris and I was eager to explore the nightlife. The seasoned campaigners warned me that I would need a lot of money. However, Peter said

to me, 'Keep your eyes on the French team at the end of
the dinner and when they move out, follow them onto their
team bus – I'll see you on it.' I duly obeyed his instructions
and found myself at the back of their bus, attempting to
converse with them in my school French, which was of
course failing miserably. The bus was just about to move
off when Peter came on with their skipper, Benoit Dauga,
and we set off on a trip to remember.

The first stop was an enormous cinema in the heart of
Paris into which we all marched arm in arm. We danced
and chanted our way down the centre aisle and up onto
the stage, bringing the film to a grinding halt. The lights
throughout the cinema came on and we all immediately
started to do a high-kicking can-can, arms interlocked,
singing the 'Marseillaise'. The whole audience clapped in
rhythm to our efforts and when we finished a voice
boomed over a loudspeaker that we were the victorious
French rugby team. This produced mass applause and
cheering and we waved, interlocked arms once more and
danced off the stage and back up the centre aisle. As we
neared the exit the applause subsided, the audience
settled down, the lights dimmed and the picture began to
roll again! Once back on the bus, I marvelled at what had
just happened and thought to myself that if we had done
that in Britain there would have been a riot and the police
would probably have been called to arrest us as hooligans.
The journey took us to (and through) numerous night-
clubs at which we were given free champagne and front-
row seats if the club had a cabaret. What amazed me was
the lack of objections from any of the patrons about having
to vacate prized, and probably prebooked, seats. It was an
exhilarating way of forgetting about our defeat in the
match – even if only for a few hours.

Some critics believe that 1971 saw the best rugby
football ever played in the international championship,
but of all the games played in that year, the match
between Scotland and Wales at Murrayfield will be re-
membered for ever. We were written off by everyone

before this game. Wales came with all their super-stars. J.P.R., Gerald, John Dawes, Barry John, Gareth, Merve the Swerve, Big Delme Thomas. As usual the crowd was a sellout and Peter's team talk was short and to the point. 'We must have confidence in our own ability and take the game to them by attacking at every opportunity, right from the start.' He was followed by Bill Dickinson, who that season had been appointed 'adviser to the captain'. Bill had come into the squad quietly at first, winning the confidence of the players with his approach, but this time he let rip. He added the cream to Peter's talk and we took the field with a feeling of great confidence and a determination to surrender nothing. The ding-dong battle which ensued, with the lead changing hands many times, is now history, but it is worthwhile recording some facts relating to the score, 19–18 in favour of Wales. We were awarded a penalty just outside our 25-yard line very early in the match, but instead of putting the ball safely into touch around the halfway line, as would normally have been the case at this stage of a game, Peter called for us to move the ball quickly to the backs. It took the Welsh (and the world!) by surprise and we broke through their defences and drove the game to deep inside their 25. The crowd jumped to their feet ecstatic at such boldness and they never sat down again.

The pulsating game was hard, fair and far-ranging. The memory of Clive Rowland's catastrophic match in 1963 at Murrayfield, when the ball was out of play longer than it was in play, was buried for ever. It was ironic that Clive was now Wales' coach and such was his joy at winning that after the match he joined the whole Welsh team in the bath – fully clothed!

As we entered injury time with Scotland having again regained the lead, Wales fought their way back into our 25 to a line-out. It was our throw and as a winger Billy Steele fetched the ball, Peter moved up from his normal position at the back of the line-out to three. He moved me to five and Alistair McHarg to eight. Delme Thomas followed

Peter (as we had hoped), Mervyn Davies stayed with Alistair at the tail, thus leaving me marked by Mike Roberts in the middle. Dunky Paterson, our scrum half, was responsible for relaying the line-out codes on Peter's instructions, but on receiving my code for the throw he rejected it, giving Peter's code instead. He shouted to Peter, 'Keep it tight, keep it tight!' Peter again instructed Dunky to give my code and turned away to prepare himself for his supporting role. Dunky stuck to his guns. By now Billy Steele was poised to throw the ball in and had picked up Peter's code from Dunky. In the hubbub Peter could not hear me screaming to him that it was his code. Billy duly threw the ball to him. An unsuspecting Peter was easily beaten to the ball by an alert Delme. The ball flew from Gareth Edwards to Barry John and on, till it reached Gerald Davies, who literally bulletted round fullback Smith to score a try which brought the score to Scotland 18, Wales 17. Peter was blazing at Billy Steele for getting, as he thought, the codes so wrong, but then realized what had happened when I angrily wanted to remonstrate with Dunky. In order to relieve my frustrations I seriously considered an early charge at John Taylor as he prepared to attempt the conversion. He was going through his normal relaxed routine and I wanted to upset that! I wanted him to have more time to think about the importance of the kick and maybe the added pressure might waver him a wee bit. I chickened out – it really was not the done thing! He kicked the goal – Joe McPartlin called it the greatest conversion since St Paul – and it won the match. The Welsh faithful went home with more than just a present for the wife. In the dressing room after the game my immense disappointment at defeat soon made way for a feeling of tremendous satisfaction of at least having participated in such a wonderful game. Much later that evening during the revelry in the North British Hotel my feeling of pride regarding the match was so strong that for a moment I had difficulty remembering who had won and who had lost.

It was in that same remarkable year, 1971, that I played my first game against England at Twickenham. This was my first visit to the hallowed home of *the* Rugby Union. We had not won a game there since 1938 when Wilson Shaw led us triumphantly. Could we lay the bogey? Despite having already lost that season to France, Ireland and Wales we had much more confidence about our chances than anyone gave us credit for.

Peter surpassed himself at the team talk. It was held in a tiny room of the hotel where we lunched – a far cry from the usual 'barn' which housed the team, reserves, coach, selectors, doctors, physiotherapist and bus driver, all of whom seemed always to be present. In this small room the atmosphere was right. The feeling was right. We were all mates together. The tension was natural. Peter did not say too much. His *pièce de résistance* was to produce his Scottish cap from its original box along with his first Scotland jersey, still carefully folded. He told us of his pride in winning these trophies and we all knew exactly what he meant. We all knew exactly how we felt and we all knew exactly what we were going to do about it!

I had never played at Twickenham before and when I ran out onto the field, an awesome feeling came over me. What was it about this place? It looked so cold and dreich. Forbidding, that is what it was. I was glad for the match to start, so I could concentrate on the job that we had to do.

England played like men possessed. They played as if they were really invincible. How on earth did Bob Hiller get up from fullback to score that try? And when will he stop kicking at goal from everywhere on the field? Who is this guy Nigel Horton? He seems to have some insatiable desire to plough backwards and forwards all over me. Thank God his partner Peter Larter is such a nice bloke, otherwise I would never survive the match. And survival was of the utmost importance. Bill Dickinson, our coach, had pointed out to me that the British Lions selectors, all of whom were sitting in the stand, would not be interested in anyone who did not have the capacity to compete and survive.

Inevitably, Big Nigel and I had a set-to and for a change it was he who needed the restorative properties of the magic sponge. The trouble was that the English sponge was already being used on John Pullin, so on rushed the Scottish physiotherapist. Sorry about the added work-load, Dad. Big Nigel was not amused!

With ten minutes to go we were losing 15–8 and the game had gone very much against us. Standing behind the posts, waiting for the attempted conversion of England's last try, my brother Peter harangued us all. He pleaded with us for an even greater effort. (We would have to score twice. It seemed impossible.) He reminded us of what he had said before the match. He reminded us of the feeling we had in the small hotel room. Suddenly scoring twice did not seem so impossible after all.

A great try by Dunky Paterson and a try by Chris Rea brought us to within a point of England. Peter had to convert Chris's try for us to win. The kick was halfway out, to the left of the posts. *Come on, Peter!* I've seen you kick that kind of goal hundreds of times. On the beach at Troon. At Marr College. At West. At Murrayfield. Just do it once more! Never mind the usual act of turning your back and walking away from the ball and blowing your nose all over the place. *Just kick the goal.* Please! Oh no! He's turned his back on it. He's blowing his nose. Doesn't he know time's nearly up? He's blowing his nose again! God, he's actually enjoying it! *Bang!* It's over. I love him. I sprint towards him to kiss him as I have never kissed him before. He pushes me away, screaming, 'We've still got a few minutes more to get through.'

We did get through and then I gave him his kiss! The pitch was swarming with Scottish fans. A marvellous mayhem – I loved it. I looked for Big Nigel. I stretched out my hand towards him but he knocked it away, glowering at me and saying, 'I'll see you next week.' He was referring of course to the centenary international between England

and Scotland due to take place at Murrayfield the following Saturday. My eternal gratitude went out to the English selection committee of the time. They saved my life. They dropped Big Nigel! Before that happened, though, came the news of the selection of the British Lions team to tour New Zealand. I was in my office when Peter phoned me. He said, 'Hello, brother, how does it feel to be a British Lion?'

'Whaaat?' I shouted down the phone at him.

'You're in the Lions team – congratulations!' he shouted back. It was one of the happiest phone calls I had ever had from Peter and it certainly made up for the beauty I had from him the previous year when he told me that Scotland had dropped me in favour of him. I am sure that Peter would have been selected for the Lions tour, too, if he had been available. Telegrams, letters, phone calls and good wishes flooded in from all parts and I was on top of the world.

It was a cock-a-hoop Scotland team (exactly the same team as that responsible for the previous week's victory at Twickenham) which took the field at Murrayfield. After being introduced to HRH the Prince of Wales, we all set about the task of 'getting stuck into the English' – the war cry of most nationalistic Scotsmen. We were a goal up within half a minute. John Spencer dropped a pass on his own goal line, following Bob Hiller's diagonal run inside his own 25 from our deep kick-off. Poor 'Spanner' claimed later that he neither expected nor saw the pass coming. John Frame, Scotland's centre, did and he pounced on the ball to score. Because of a slightly early kick-off many Scots supporters missed that try and could not believe their eyes when they glanced at the scoreboard for the first time. The game started badly for England and deteriorated for them from then on. We hammered them soundly by 26 to 6, scoring five tries in the process. It could have been ten!

Troon was just as delighted at the success of the Brown brothers as we were and both Peter and I accepted

invitations to attend a function in the Troon Council
Chambers. At this, the Troon Town Council very kindly
presented to us both, on behalf of the general public of
Troon, mementoes 'in appreciation of the services ren-
dered to Troon, not only in respect of rugby, but in a more
general and sporting sense'. The mementoes were beautiful gold cufflinks bearing the town's coat of arms. A
unique gift which, along with the thought behind it, was
sincerely appreciated by Peter and me. The original gift
was to have been a gold watch, suitably inscribed, but on
checking with the Scottish Rugby Union, the Town Clerk
was advised that a gift of that value would infringe our
amateur status!

Later that day Peter and I were the guests of Marr
College. We each made a speech to the whole school, a
quite daunting experience, and also presented an auto-
graphed ball from the Marr FP's inaugural match plus
some international jerseys. It was a very proud day for
both Peter and me but, I think, even more so for my
parents who were present both at the Council Chambers
and at Marr College.

The next day I received a letter from Tom Tweedie, the
secretary of Marr Rugby Club, inviting me to accept
honorary life membership of the club. I felt very honoured
indeed and, of course, I accepted. Peter also received the
same honour.

Peter enjoyed playing rugby immensely. There were
few dull moments when he was around. He had quite an
array of trademarks: heading the ball; cotton wool bunged
up both nostrils, to stem the flow of blood from his regular
nosebleeds; enormous reverse cross-field passes; turning
his back on balls he was just about to kick over the bar; the
amazing flight trajectory of his goal-kicks. One kick at the
the Colombes Stadium, Paris, dipped, curled, tumbled and
soared on its way to clear the bar successfully. It was described perfectly by Norman Mair: 'A ballistic miracle'.

Peter was a very clean player and was rarely involved in
any untoward scenes at any level of the game. One

140

incident, though, which is still vivid in my mind was when J. P. R. Williams, the Welsh fullback, stamped on Peter's head after they had both landed in touch together following Peter's tackle on J.P.R. The incident was witnessed by the whole stand but not by the referee or most of the Scottish team. J.P.R. therefore escaped official punishment. But he received unofficial punishment two minutes later when Dunky Paterson, our scrum half, hoisted a beautiful up-and-under to him. With all of us sprinting like mad to get to the target area he had no chance – and he knew it! He was flattened and pulverized by us all, but after receiving some prolonged attention by the sponge man, he returned to the fray as if nothing had happened. That was J.P.R.! Fate dealt with him later in the game when he broke his jaw after an accidental collision with our flying winger Billy Steele.

The assault left Peter concussed. He did not have a clue about what was going on – and he was the skipper! We completely lost our rhythm and despite pleas from my father (from the touch line) and myself to go off the field, Peter insisted that he was all right and remained for the rest of the match. That was not the sole reason for our awful defeat but as in those days every team was up against it so much anyway at the National Stadium, Cardiff, it was a hindrance we could have well done without.

J.P.R. made a very dramatic reappearance midway through the after-match dinner in the Angel Hotel with his mouth and jaw wired up. He later headed for the top table to seek out Peter and after exchanging a few words, they both departed the scene. I was taking great interest in these goings-on; curiosity and concern got the better of me, so after waiting ten seconds I dived out of the door after them.

I found them in the corner of the large but empty bar. They were in deep discussion. I kept myself out of their view until they finally broke out of their conclave and shook hands. I felt incredible relief at this sight and broke my cover to join them to find out what the hell was going on. J.P.R. immediately came to me and, in what was for him a very emotional manner, explained that he had been apologizing profusely to Peter about his assault on him and that he had no idea at all what had come over him to make him do it! He then apologized to me for assaulting Peter, who was nodding to me in the background his obvious acceptance of the apology. J.P.R. and I embraced and we all returned to the dinner together.

A typical example of the fun, flair and humour which Peter possessed, and displayed on the field of play, occurred during the Scotland versus All Blacks game in 1972. The All Blacks had a drop-out 25. I was standing on the touch-line on the stand side, with Peter about fifteen yards infield and twenty yards downfield from me. As we awaited the kick, he called out to me above the din, 'If it's a high-hanging ball, I'll come forward and head it, so you be prepared to run on to it.' Knowing Peter as I did, I knew that he meant it! No sooner had I organized myself than the All Blacks stand-off Stevens turned away from Peter and blootered the ball upfield to Andy Irvine. As Peter and I ran back into defence, he looked at me over his shoulder and shouted, 'The bugger must have heard me.' He was not to be outdone, however; just before full time he rose to catch a chip ahead from the opposition and at the last second, sensing that he might receive the whole All Blacks pack on top of him at the same time, he headed the ball safely into touch! Amid the hubbub and tension of the resultant line-out, I thought to myself, 'That'll be sixpence I owe him!'

As I left the dressing room to board the team bus a long time after full time, I was greeted by a wee boy who said that he had been waiting there all that time just for me. He was the only one left from the throng who had earlier been pouncing eagerly on my more punctual team mates. He was wet and cold and he implored me to sign my autograph on his sodden match programme despite the many shouts of, 'Hurry up, Broonie,' which were emanating from the team bus. As I peeled the pages open he said to me excitedly, 'You were great today, I've never seen such a magnificent display before. Your line-out jumping and timing were first class, your rucking was incredible and you covered every blade of grass on that pitch out there.' Proudly, I was just about to sign, when he blurted out, 'Keep it up, Peter!' I humbly moved my pen away from my photo to Peter's and reluctantly signed 'Peter C. Brown'. It's a great life!

The Scotland versus SRU President's XV game in 1973, arranged to celebrate the SRU's centenary year, marked Peter's retirement from international rugby. He certainly left his mark on the game, not only with his adroit ability but also with his unexpected ploys and tactics. We owe much to him for his part in launching the 'Scotland Winning Machine' of the early seventies at Murrayfield and for his attacking ideas which, even if a little bizarre, always made the crowd and his opponents sit up and take notice. He had probably the greatest spring jump of all the players I have seen. His innovative ideas, allied to those of Bill Dickinson, had Scotland leading the way in the world of short penalty routines – routines that worked. My favourite was the 'Jumbo' move of the early seventies which saw us all charging on criss-cross runs off Ian McLauchlan as pivot. I loved it when my code was called and Ian plonked the ball into my midriff, allowing me to launch myself full tilt into the heart of the opposition. Just before starting my run-up I always used to pick out an opposing player fifteen yards or so beyond Ian and I always would say to myself, You're going to run through him. There was the odd occasion when I set off on a dummy run and got absolutely flattened. When that happened, I always consoled myself with the thought that at least I made a convincing decoy.

I received thirty caps for Scotland, three more than Peter. But one statistic on which he hammers me is the number of tries scored for Scotland. Despite dreaming about it hundreds of times, the reality is that I never scored once. Whereas Peter scored three – and all against England!

Peter was a superb sevens player and was a member of the very successful Gala team which, in the early to mid seventies in particular, had a virtual monopoly of the Border sevens trophies and medals.

I took a seven from West of Scotland to Melrose, the home of sevens rugby and *the* tournament of the circuit. We were taken little notice of even although we won our first-round tie against Jedforest, a stuffy Border side. Our opponents in the next round were Gala – Peter and all! Gala were the red-hot favourites, having won the trophy for the last three years. In the first-round tie they had disposed of a super Melrose seven most capably and you just couldn't get odds for us at all from anyone.

We geared ourselves for the game of our lives and ignored the awesome task ahead of us. Polite but sympathetic applause greeted us as we ran out onto the field. We would normally have been cheered by the Hawick supporters, but with their team having been hammered in the first round by Rosslyn Park (Englishmen at that!) they were all away to the Melrose hostelries to drown their sorrows. Gala were welcomed by a deafening roar! Hamish Biggar kicked off – a lovely high, hanging ball which landed right where Peter was standing. I arrived just as he reached up to catch it and I absolutely obliterated him. (If my mother had been in the stand that day she would have passed out.) We quickly gained possession and in no time opened up a gap for Bryan Gossman to sprint away to score.

It took Peter a wee while to recover from my boneshaker and as he was normally the greatest source of ball for the Gala team, they were struggling all the way. We clinched the game by 18 points to 0. After that tie there was not much room to be found inside the Melrose hostelries. Gala and Hawick supporters commiserating together? The mind boggles.

Peter and I had a fair old tussle in the line-outs that day, but I had the last laugh. At a line-out on the halfway in front of the stand, Gala threw the ball in but I did not contest the throw this time, thereby allowing Peter a completely free jump. I then burst through and intercepted his unsuspecting tap back before it reached the Gala scrum half. My momentum took me away up field and I was tackled only a few yards short of the line by Colin Gass. Ron Watt, however, was at my elbow and he took my inside pass to romp home triumphantly round behind the posts. What a try. What a day. What a brother!

10

'C'est magnifique, mais ce n'est pas la guerre'

Rugby players, and not only the younger ones, do some incredibly stupid things to play in matches while they are injured so seriously that, for their own good, they should never be allowed anywhere near the ground. The trouble is that the player concerned always wants to play so badly that he sets himself the goal of achieving fitness by a certain date, and he just will not accept that, when the times comes, he has not recovered. I have done it so often that I ought to have had my head examined, and yet I never seemed to learn. I never stopped to work out that almost every time I did this and played when I should not have played, I aggravated the injury in question so much that I played myself out of far more football, and missed a far greater number of games, than I would have done if I had accepted the realities of the injury in the first place.

Still, I was not alone, and perhaps the best, or the worst, example of that was Ian McLauchlan's determination to play in the match between England and Scotland at Twickenham in 1973, even though he had broken his leg only two weeks previously in the match against Ireland. By then Ian had been made captain of Scotland, and the team was seeking its fifth victory in succession, and with it the Triple Crown for the first time since 1938.

The truth was that Ian should never have been in London, let alone leading Scotland into battle, but his determination to play was fierce. His stubborn, burning fanaticism eventually warded off the committee's feeble efforts to make him stand down. I believe that Ian honestly felt that he could do the job that he was selected for and not let anybody down, least of all himself, in the process. Nevertheless he was only a shadow of his normal self on the day and the team definitely suffered because of it. It would be totally belittling every other performance for Scotland that Ian played to say otherwise. He was undoubtedly the best scrummager I ever played behind and I am an authority on his performances because I was behind him in Argentina, South Africa, New Zealand, Australia, France, Wales, England, Ireland and numerous paddocks throughout Scotland. His workrate in the line-outs (as a blocker, of course!) and in the loose was immense, but at Twickenham he demanded too much from his body.

Scotland did not lose the match because of Ian McLauchlan; there were many question marks hanging over other players' fitness levels that same day. Some players too must look to their consciences and admit that they had accepted defeat long before full time. Just after half time, I came on as substitute, replacing Jock Millican, the Edinburgh University wing forward, and I know who responded, who tried, and who did not. 'Cometh the hour, cometh the man' is a great saying and there is no finer stage than the rugby field for its true meaning to be demonstrated.

I knew that I would be on the field some time during the game. It was not a psychic feeling; it was based purely on reality. There was so much attention focused on Ian McLauchlan's leg before the game that the dubious fitness levels of at least five other members of the pack were never investigated. No one noticed that on the Friday Nairn MacEwan, our wing forward from Gala, took no part whatsoever in the training session because of a groin injury. Our team dressing room looked like a casualty ward *before* the match. All in all, six members of the pack were receiving pain-killing injections of some

147

sort, somewhere! I do not know whether the backs were fit. I was too scared to inquire!

As I took my seat in the stand along with the other substitutes, I was wrapped up to the nines. I was so hot, in fact, that I was perspiring, and John Frame, the Gala centre (what a superb class of substitute Scotland had that day!) said to me, 'What are you so hot and bothered about?' My reply was short and to the point. 'Because there is no way I don't get on the park today.' Just at that a voice boomed out over the Tannoy system, 'If there is a doctor present, would he kindly make his way to the main entrance immediately.' I thought to myself, I doubt the Scottish doctor can't cope down there and he needs a hand.

Just before half time my brother Peter was in the wars and looked as if he would have to come off, so I dashed downstairs and down the tunnel to the side of the pitch in readiness. However, he recovered sufficiently to continue. My feelings were mixed because I obviously didn't want him to be hurt badly, and I was also disappointed that I had not been called onto the field. I was desperate to become involved, especially since we were losing by 14 points to 3 and, in racing terms, England were going away from us.

I did not return to my seat in the grandstand as I felt that I would be making a return journey in no time if I did. I took a seat beside my father (still the team physio) in the enclosure beside the pitch from where I could scream my head off at the boys to try to encourage them as much as possible. Fond hope! We were not winning enough of the ball to do anything about the stranglehold England had over us, and our scrummaging was the poorest I had seen it for years.

At that point, Jock Millican was concussed after a collision with the whole English pack and was led off the field. It was ironic that Jock had to come off because he was one of the two players who had not required pain-killing injections before the match! I jumped up onto the pitch and greeted Jock sympathetically. But I was wasting my time, his eyes were rolling into the top of his head and he had no idea what was happening.

I immediately said to the English doctor, 'I can go on right away then, sir?'

He replied quite indignantly, 'I'll have to examine him first of all.'

Examine him? Examine him? I demanded to myself. There's no way that guy's ever going back on. That assumption was not based on my having passed my Tenderfoot first-aid test during my short sortie into the Boy Scouts in Troon in my early teens, but on the fact that I know someone in cloud cuckooland when I see him!

I ran up and down the touchline stretching my muscles as much as possible before launching into battle. I was becoming almost hysterical over the seemingly inexplicable delay in pronouncing Jock unfit to resume playing. I had no need to build up my adrenaline because it had been pumping furiously ever since the match kicked off. After what seemed like a week in Eastbourne, Bill Dickinson finally came running down the tunnel shooing me onto the field. I did not need a second telling.

I could not believe how low in spirits some of the forwards were. It was as if they had been playing for a week against world-beaters and knew that no matter what they tried they were wasting their time. I ran about screaming and bawling at them all – at my brother, too. I even struck some of them in an attempt to get a response! The main reaction came from Peter and Alistair McHarg, and we started to win much more line-out ball for the backs to use. In no time at all, Billy Steele had scored two tries, one of which Andy Irvine converted to bring the score to 14–13 for England. This set the game alight and I honestly felt that we were going to do it. The play was fast and furious and the crowd were on the edge of their seats as we pressed for the winning score. But it was not to be. Billy Steele, David Duckham and Andy Irvine all chased a high ball into our in-goal area and as Billy elected to allow the ball one bounce before smothering it, it cruelly eluded him and the other two. Unfortunately for us, the next man up in support was Geoff Evans, the Coventry centre, and he gleefully accepted the presentation to score the match-sealing try. Goodbye, Triple Crown, once again!

But having criticized Ian McLauchlan, I must confess that earlier that season, I had been guilty of displaying just the same stubborn, fanatical determination to play for Scotland when, instead, I should have been at home with my ankle in plaster. The game was against New Zealand in December 1972. That season was Scotland's centenary and in October I was proud to take part in the Scotland/Ireland versus England/Wales celebration game which was riddled with glorious attacking rugby. I was over-joyed at winning and very happy with my own form. Thereafter, my mind was focused on one thing and one thing only – the All Blacks. I was eating, sleeping, drinking and living the fixture. It was, I suppose, unhealthy. But having gone through all the traumas of New Zealand with the Lions the previous year, I just could not wait to get at them in my own backyard.

Imagine my despondency when I damaged ankle ligaments in the last few minutes of the national trial only two weeks before the game. I was beside myself with anguish. I was terrified of missing the game because playing in it meant so very much to me. It was an obsession. I received treatment daily from both Hugh Allan, the Kilmarnock Football Club phsyiotherapist, and my father, meanwhile exercising as much and as hard as possible. I declared myself fit for the match.

I met the team on the Thursday as usual and the whole session went well for me until, late on, we started rucking practice. I went over on my ankle and the searing pain was hellish. I limped off the field into the dressing room in tears – my world seemed to have collapsed about me. I returned to the hotel and barricaded myself in my bedroom to immerse my ankle in buckets of ice. I did not want to have to admit that I was unfit to play. All the inquiries from committee members and other people about my fitness I warded off by saying, 'It's a bit sore, but we'll see what it's like in the morning.' I kept my ankle raised all night, and in the morning the swelling had gone down amazingly. I told my room mate, Alistair McHarg, to explain to the selectors that I was not training that morning because of a slight cold. While the team trained at Murrayfield, I hid in my bedroom all morning with my ankle raised as high as possible to further alleviate the swelling. That afternoon my father arrived at the hotel to set up office for the players' massage, etc., and he immediately called at my room to see me. One look at my ankle and my restricted movement and he said firmly, 'There's no way you can play tomorrow.' Ignoring my protestations, he disappeared and returned almost at once with my brother Peter, who was skipper of the team. Peter said quietly that, much as he and the team needed me, there was no way I was playing and that he was going to tell the selectors accordingly. Well, that was like a red rag to a bull. 'I'll show you,' I bellowed stubbornly after him as he loped off down the stairs. There was soon a steady procession of selectors knocking at my door to ascertain the full facts. Although they then summoned a replacement (Ron Wright of Edinbugh Wanderers) for me, I successfully negotiated one last chance by obsessively insisting that if I were given pain-killing injections just before the kick-off I would be capable of performing for eighty minutes as originally planned. Bloody crazy, wasn't I?

We filled two cars and set off for the Royal Infirmary in Edinburgh, where on arrival I received some pain-killing injections in my ankle. I then proceeded to demonstrate to the selectors present, the doctors, my father, my brother and Bill Dickinson that I could jump up and down and that I could run flat out. I sprinted up and down the middle of a ward in which the patients wondered what in the name of goodness was going on. When I finished, I asked the doctor outright, 'Can you give me enough pain-killers to last eighty minutes?' The answer was in the affirmative. I then turned to my 'execution squad' and spouted, 'There's no problem then, is there?' I walked out of the door to the car before anyone could answer otherwise!

My ploy succeeded! We all travelled back to the hotel and I went to bed to rest for the game the next day, but I did not sleep too well because my ankle was so sore. All the time I was awake my father's words kept ringing in my ears: 'No matter what else you manage tomorrow, you'll definitely succeed in damaging your ankle ligaments. You mustn't play.' I discounted future problems because all I wanted, in the whole world, was to play against the All Blacks – and especially against Peter Whiting.

When I awoke next morning, I jumped out of bed to pull back the curtains to check the weather and nearly passed out with the searing pain which shot up my leg. I gasped so loudly at the shock to my system that I disturbed the slumber of Alistair McHarg. I limped back to my bed in agony, almost unable to put my weight on my foot at all. 'Jesus Christ, Broonie,' said Big Al, 'have you really been passed fit to play?' I confirmed that I had and attempted to dispel his concern. I had breakfast in bed and warded off another plea from Peter for me not to play. He said to me emotively, 'Of course I want you on the park today, but not at the expense of the rest of the season.' Still totally obsessed with my goal I replied, 'I must play today.' I think that he wanted to punch me between the eyes in a last-ditch effort to bring me to my senses. I now wish that he had!

I ate my pre-match special lunch in my bedroom because I did not want to spread fear and alarm within the team over my obvious lameness. I hirpled down to the team room later to attend the captain's talk, a journey which I just about managed. I was quiet on the trip to Murrayfield. I did not join in the singing as much as I would normally because of my growing concern about my actions. Once inside the ground, the bus eased its way through the crowd to the home team entrance. Now I had to negotiate the ten or twelve yards between the bus and the entrance door without the public noticing my predicament. My fellow players crowded around me as I left the bus, camouflaging me perfectly. Once safe inside the dressing room, I knew that I was going to make it – I was going to play against the All Blacks at Murrayfield! (Even now, I cannot believe how pigheaded I was.)

While Peter was giving his last team talk just two minutes before we took the field, I was on the physio's couch having pain-killing injections pumped into my ankle at all angles. When he finished giving me the needle, the SRU surgeon, Jimmy Thomson, said, 'Gordon, that lot should see you through the dance tonight, never mind the next eighty-odd minutes.' That was exactly what I wanted!

I do not think that by playing while injured my contribution was impaired, or that I played other than well, but then that's what Ian McLauchlan felt after his Twickenham efforts! I still feel embarrassed at what I did.

I did make the dance that night, but I did not play any rugby for the next two months. I seriously damaged my ankle ligaments (of course!) by playing with the aid of pain-killers and that cost me three possible caps. I missed Scotland's defeat in Paris and our two victories at Murrayfield against Wales and Ireland.

There was one injury I played with for the whole of my rugby career, a damaged shoulder. One day at Troon swimming pool, when I was a teenager, I was going through my usual gambit of showing off to the young ladies by diving off the top diving board, which was eighteen feet high, into nine feet of water, and then plummeting down the big shute on my knees and diving off at the bottom at great speed into only three feet of water. Sounds crazy, doesn't it? Well, I was so busy fooling around on the big shute that I lost my concentration. Instead of skimming across the surface of the water when I dived off at the bottom, I went straight under, crashing at speed into the tiled bottom of the pool. I managed to surface and stand up, then I noticed that the water around me was red. I realized that it was blood from my head. I had split it open. A girl standing at the poolside screamed and fainted. Some swimmers helped me out of the water. My injuries looked awful because, as I was so wet, the blood was flowing freely down me. I was more concerned with the searing pain coming from my right shoulder. I could not move my arm at all. I was rushed to hospital and had my head stitched and my arm put in a plaster. I had smashed the tip of my shoulder, damaging it in such a way that I could never again reach as high with my right arm as I could with my left. This was to dictate my line-out jumping options for the rest of my life.

My first piece of real stupidity in playing while injured was during my first season in senior rugby. I was playing for Glasgow against Edinburgh (the Inter-City) and it was the first game I had ever played in that was televised (on BBC 2's 'Rugby Special'). Just before half time we went for a pushover try from a 5-yard scrum and something happened to my right knee. It was a displacement of some sort. The pain was not too severe so I carried on for a few minutes, but as I could not straighten my knee at all, I was advised to go off for a proper diagnosis. The doctor immediately espied a displaced cartilage and said that my rugby was over, not just for the afternoon but for some time to come, until it was rested and restored. My father, who was at the match as a spectator, came round to the dressing room to see how I was. On examining me, he completely agreed with the diagnosis. Now I had listened to all this chat with one ear and to the roar of the crowd with the other. My heart was thumping to get back into action despite the knee. Just then Rodney Balfour, our hooker, was led into the dressing room suffering from concussion. That meant that our pack was down to six and there were no substitutes in those days. As all the attention shifted to Rodney I said to no one in particular, 'I'm going out to stretch my legs,' and slipped out of the dressing room. Once outside I immediately pushed my way through the crowds and, after attracting the referee's attention, limped back onto the field.

I am told it was some minutes before I was missed from the dressing room and, of course, by that time it was too late for anyone to do anything about it. No one would have come onto the pitch and stopped the game to yank me off for my own good. Thankfully, I do not think there would be any hesitation nowadays, no matter who's concerned. By stupidly reappearing on the pitch I proceeded to tear the already damaged cartilage. A bitter pill was given to me to swallow two days later: An immediate cartilage operation and three months off rugby! I was heartbroken but realistically accepted that it was my own fault for acting as I did during the Inter-City. There are no prizes for guessing what my father said to me about ignoring the diagnosis in the dressing room!

The operation at Kilmarnock Infirmary was successfully carried out ten days after the Inter-City by Mr Rae Simpson, the chairman, as I write, of Rangers FC. I did not mind too much being admitted to hospital as a patient for the first time. The pain and discomfort I accepted as punishment in part for my foolishness. Part of hospital life which drove me crazy, though, was the goings-on between one of the night nurses from another ward and one of the patients on my ward. I didn't sleep too well after the operation and that was when I made my observations. She would slip into the ward sometime between 1.30 and 3 a.m., stealthily make her way to the top of the ward and silently pull the curtains round the patient's bed to conceal their fun and games. She never stayed longer than half an hour but he still had a big grin on his face at breakfast time!

Despite the speedy operation my muscle wastage was quite frightening, and the long road back to full fitness seemed to extend to the horizon and beyond. I was lucky that my father was at hand to assist and guide me throughout my recovery period and thereby accelerated my progress.

One of the exercises I had to do was quad tightening and leg raising every hour for five minutes. I disciplined myself to do this even though it did lead to some embarrassing moments, especially when I returned to work at the bank where I was a teller. Despite the queues, the customers' glares, and my poor colleagues' utterings, I sat down in my teller's box and did my five minutes' sweat – one has to be selfish if one wants to be successful!

Receiving pain-killing injections in my shoulder was quite a common occurrence during my career – especially on tours. My first tour was with Scotland to Argentina in 1969 and having damaged my shoulder in the first game I had to receive injections in my shoulder to enable me to play in my second game. The game at Rosario was the only one of the six which was played outside Buenos Aires. Rosario is the birthplace of Che Guevara, the well-known guerrilla fighter and cult hero, and the local team had many players who seemed to desire to follow in his violent footsteps. Our stay in Rosario was bizarre from start to finish! During our first training session, bombs started exploding nearby, sending us scurrying into the dressing room for safety. We later found out that impatient strikers at the massive local beef factory had rioted. We were whipped away to a club on the outskirts of the city where all was quiet and relaxed – that is, until we were paid a visit by a poisonous snake whilst eating our barbecue lunch. I think that was the fastest I ever moved during the whole tour! All afternoon we watched palls of black smoke spiral and climb into the sky. Occasionally a bomb blast was heard.

We ventured cautiously back into the city centre later that day with some local rugby union officials acting as scouts riding ahead of our bus on scooters. On the way we passed burned-out buses, trains, bus depots, railway stations, shops, offices and banks. It was very eerie and the general consensus was that we should get the hell back to Buenos Aires as soon as possible! We reached our hotel safely and were immediately advised that the airport was closed, no trains were running, no buses were to be allowed beyond the city boundaries – in other words, there was no escape! A curfew was immediately introduced by the army and yet we still kept our rendezvous that night at a cocktail party at the local businessmen's club. We had to walk to the club in twos, leaving the hotel at two-minute intervals. I did not enjoy the five-minute walk one bit. The evening had a terrible cloud hanging over it because we all knew that the return journey had to be made. My last memory of that club was the waiters chasing, and crunching underfoot, giant cockroaches. I would be just about to plonk a mouthful of food where it belonged when – crunch! – another cockroach would bite the dust. I did not eat very much.

The game against Rosario was postponed for twenty-four hours to await the outcome of the rioting, during which eight rioters died. Sandy Carmichael, Frank Laidlaw and I sneaked onto the roof of the hotel to sunbathe. From our vantage point we could hear gunfire some way off and could see fires that were the aftermath of recent bombings. Then two army helicopters started hovering above our heads. It was all very exciting, but our sunning and excitement was soon brought to an end when we were advised by the management to get the hell off the roof before the soldiers in the helicopters thought we were snipers and started shooting at *us*!

The game was played after the twenty-four-hour postponement. Although the rioting in the city had ceased, it was re-enacted on the field! The violence was quite incredible – even the backs were dishing it out to us. The first game of the tour, which I thought was quite rough, was a kids' party compared with this one. Rosario's second-row partners were the Suarez twins. One of them was psychopathic, the other was on the level, but because they were identical they were both hammered just to make sure. During the general mayhem we actually played some stirring, if brave, rugby and were eventually convincing winners. The local referee was conspicuous by his absence. Maybe there were some future guerilla leaders present at the match – talent spotting!

During the tour I received constant treatment to my damaged shoulder but near the end of the trip I was badly burned when I was left alone too long on a deep-heat machine. The situation was ludicrous: because there were so many wires and cables around my body I could not move an inch and I shouted for ages before I was finally set free. The electrical burn took almost three months to heal properly.

I suffered pains in my neck and down my arms for the whole domestic season following the Lions' South Africa tour of 1974. But, as usual, I ignored them and continued playing. I was captain of West of Scotland and was desperate to have a championship-winning side. The championship was hardly under way when I broke my thumb tackling a Dunfermline player. I had to stop then.

During my enforced break the pain in my neck eased. My frustrations as skipper were not helped by the ever increasing injury list that depleted my first XV squad. Three defeats in a row also brought the threat of relegation too close for comfort. So I returned to the fray as soon as possible, in time for our game at home against Hawick, who were at that time on top of the league.

We totally outplayed them in the forwards. We played eight-and-a-half-man rugby, only giving the ball to the scrum half now and then. By denying them any possession we snuffed out the threat of their back division, which was exceptional at that time, with Jim Renwick the star attraction. Why he was not selected for South Africa is a mystery. We were leading by 6 points to 0 going into the last few minutes of the game. The thought of 2 points for a win and therefore safety from relegation were foremost in my mind. Then, Jim Renwick received his first pass of the day. From deep inside his own half he set off at speed, dodging and weaving his way through our defences. He eventually broke clear with only our fullback Keith Martin to beat. He had his winger outside him in the overlap. As I covered back desperately with my heart in my mouth

I saw Keith line him up. Bang! The tackle was made, just as I had seen Keith do for years at Marr, but the ball was away and the try was scored in the corner. It was 6 points to 4 with the conversion still to come. Jim Renwick took a long time to get to his feet. The tackle by Keith had made its mark. Eventually he recovered sufficiently to attempt the conversion but he failed and the points were ours.

The pains in my neck continued right through the international season including the victory over Wales at Murrayfield. We won by 12 points to 10 and the game was watched by a record crowd of a 104,000, although I think 120,000 people actually gained access to Murrayfield that day.

The pain in my arm was becoming so bad that I could not sleep at night. It was touch and go whether I would play in the Irish centenary match. I played and suffered the consequences. I was in agony after it.

The game, which Ireland/Scotland won comfortably, was disappointing and bad-tempered. This was a great pity because before the match the spirits of everyone were excellent. Fortunately, Eamonn Andrews was waiting for Willie John McBride as he left the field, and Willie John's 'This Is Your Life' recording got the evening's celebrations off to a good start, thus relieving the tension in the air.

I had my neck X-rayed and then examined by a neurologist. It seemed I had damaged a disc in my neck and the nerves down my arm were being affected. I was advised that the full result of the tests would not be known for two or three days. Linda and I travelled down to the Lake District for a long weekend holiday and it was from there that I telephoned the doctor for the diagnosis.

'Complete rest for three months,' he said, 'otherwise serious problems may occur.'

I was due to fly to New Zealand in ten days' time for a five weeks' tour with Scotland. 'I had better phone the Scottish Rugby Union right away,' I remarked.

'Don't worry,' was the reply, 'I've already informed

159

them. Bill Watson is going in your place.'

Did they really think I would go on a tour to New Zealand with a dicky neck? You bet they did! No wonder, after all the stupid things I had done to date.

In January 1976 I broke a bone in my right hand whilst playing for Glasgow against the North and Midlands at Aberdeen. My hand was kicked following my tackle on one of their centre threequarters and it was so misshapen I knew something serious had happened. My father, who was Glasgow's physiotherapist at the time, confirmed my suspicions with one gloomy shake of the head. My hand was X-rayed at Aberdeen Infirmary and, amazingly, the verdict was 'deep bruising'. I sighed with great relief, because the French international was only two weeks away.

I'd suspected something was going to happen during the game because events leading up to it were far from encouraging. The train journey north from Glasgow was bedevilled by breakdowns and stoppages. We were therefore very late in arriving in Aberdeen, which left far less time for us to unwind and prepare properly than we would have liked. My final pre-match preparation was obliterated when the referee, Jake Short of Hawick, insisted on my changing all my studs because he reckoned they were outside the legal length. I had to comply. It took me ages, and I nearly missed the kick-off because of it.

The return journey to Glasgow that night was even worse than the one in the morning. We broke down God knows how many times, and I did not get home to Troon until 3.30 a.m. I had started out from there at 6.30 a.m. the previous day! My hand was enormously swollen by this time and my father was sure that I must have fractured something. Rae Simpson, the surgeon at Kilmarnock, X-rayed my hand on the Sunday and, sure enough, he spied a fracture. I politely refused a plaster cast on my hand and wrist because that would weaken them. I wanted to have my hand as strong as possible for the French game because there was no way I was going to

160

miss it. Rae Simpson warned me of the consequences of such an action: 'Possible permanent damage if the injury receives another direct blow so soon after the original fracture.' When he realized how determined I was to play against France, he helped me over the next two weeks as much as possible to strengthen the healing fracture. Initial manipulation under X-ray, then a series of cortisone injections, was the agenda.

The Scottish selectors had other plans. At the beginning of the squad session at Murrayfield on the Sunday before the game I was called into the doctor's private room under the stand. All the selectors were present and they told me that I should call off because of my injured hand. They were concerned about the possible long-term damage I could suffer, and also that an early blow in the game would obviously affect my performance, to the detriment of everyone, myself included. I appreciated their concern, but insisted that I'd be OK and would not let them down. They were still quite adamant that I should call off and thereby be fully fit for the Welsh game at Cardiff two weeks later. I then had the audacity to say that I would call off the French match only if I was guaranteed my place for the Welsh game. I was told in no uncertain terms that no such guarantee could ever be granted to anyone (quite right!)

My reply was quite simple. 'If I call off the French match, and we beat them, you will then probably select the same team for Wales. Which means I'll be missing two internationals.' I then asked Dr Jimmy Thomson if enough pain-killer could be pumped into my hand before the French match to stave off any discomfort whatsoever, no matter how many blows connected during the game. He warned me of the obvious long-term consequences of such an action, but admitted that he could easily administer sufficient pain-killer to last the match. 'Then there's no problem, is there?' I said as I opened the door of the room, and I walked out to rejoin the rest of the team.

Throughout the squad session that day I expected

someone from 'on high' to tap me on the shoulder and say, 'Gordon, despite your stubborn determination to play – you're out.' As I later drove home to Troon along the M8 motorway I couldn't believe my luck.

I received many bangs and thumps on my hand during the game, but, true to the doc's word, I never felt a thing. My hand did not hinder me at all during the whole length of the match. Afterwards it was bloody awful. I had damaged it further, irreparably. Till my dying day I'll regret my pigheadedness in playing. My hand is weakened for ever.

We even lost the match. Mind you, the referee was to blame. Really, he was! We were all over the Frenchmen, winning plenty of ball and attacking feverishly, but we could not get the one score which, in my experience, would have made them crack up and open the flood gates. Then the score came. We kicked a penalty and the tammies were up in the air – only temporarily, though. The referee, Ken Pattinson of England, ruled that Ian McLauchlan was offside as he lay on the ground holding the ball steady in the wind for the kicker, and cancelled the goal. We fell apart at this decision, which was quite wrong, and before we knew it, the French had their tails up and sustained their advantage.

As I say, I have done some daft things through playing with injuries which I should have accepted as being serious enough to stop me playing, but the most bizarre injury of all those I received in my career was inflicted upon me, if that is the word, when I was playing for West of Scotland at Melrose. The match was very fluid, with West running up 30 points, the highest score then against Melrose in postwar years. The whole team played well with our stand-off Hamish Biggar, brother of Alastair the international, particularly outstanding. My jubilation in the dressing room afterwards was quietened somewhat by a very painful gash on my shin. I strapped up my leg and headed for home. But over the next few days the gash got wider and my left foot swelled so much that I could not wear a shoe. I eventually went to hospital for an X-ray. I was flabbergasted when the casualty doctor said to me, 'How did you get a tooth in your leg?'

'No way,' said I, 'it'll be a splinter from a metal stud.'

'We shall see then, won't we?' he replied, with a twinkle in his eye.

He gave me a local anaesthetic. Then he inserted some tweezers into the middle of the gash and, right before my eyes, extracted a human tooth, roots and all, complete with a piece of gum still attached! I could not believe it. A tooth in my leg? By this time word had spread round the hospital, and doctors and nurses were flocking to see this phenomenon. I was presented with the tooth in a small glass bottle as a macabre memento. I had limped into the hospital but strolled out, such was the instant relief of the extraction. No sooner was I home than the phone began ringing nonstop. The press were really taken by the story, which someone at the hospital must have passed on, and they all wanted to know who had bitten me or who I had kicked in the face.

By this time, of course, the question was going through my mind too, but I knew that there was no way anyone had bitten me and I certainly had not kicked anyone on the mouth. The only incident that could explain the tooth was a collision I had with the Melrose wingforward Alistair Wilson. We had both chased a long throw over a shortened line-out and as I fly-hacked the ball upfield, Alistair dived a fraction too late to smother it. He collided with the follow-through of my left leg and was knocked out in the process. I was aware of having pain in my leg at the time but I paid no special attention to it. I certainly never thought, I wonder if I've got a tooth in my leg? I still have a mark on my leg as a reminder of that day.

The press kept the story alive for over a week. The banter reported between Alistair and me seemed to appeal to the masses. One doctor was quoted as saying that I was lucky that the tooth was not decayed otherwise I would have been badly poisoned. So I, of course, was

163

thankful that Alistair had kept his teeth so healthy and clean. One dentist claimed that as the tooth had not been damaged in any way during its 'extraction' from Alistair's mouth, then it could possibly be transplanted back again. Alistair's reply was lovely. 'Tell Gordon to put it under his pillow and maybe the fairies will give him sixpence for his trouble.'

Every rugby player enjoys playing as often as possible, and as rugby is a physical-contact game, most players have a running series of bumps and bruises which tend to be ignored. It is also not normally in the make-up of players to complain too much about such ailments. However, there must come a time in every rugby player's life when the ailment requires rest and attention. Sadly, the macho side of us does not allow us to admit that we have an injury that hurts. Of course, there are other angles. We do not want to call off in case the replacement plays too well and is retained once we recover. Nor do we ever wish anyone to hang the label 'injury-prone' on our peg in the dressing room. Generally, though, I think the burning desire to keep playing without a break weighs on us most heavily, and although no one will ever thank a player for playing with an injury, and playing badly, it is always an excuse to fall back on.

I have often felt too that the feeling of letting my team mates down by not playing weighed on my shoulders. 'They'll never manage without me' is something I've told myself often – too often. 'They'll never manage to find someone to take my place' is an honest statement of concern, rather than a big-headed attitude.

When players have a dilemma over whether to play because of injury, the decision should be taken out of their hands as quickly as possible. Most of the time the major problem is getting the players to talk about injuries they are carrying. Despite the fact that rugby is such a bastion of amateurism, too often this is allowed to cloud the issue, thus putting all the onus for decision-making on the player. Few players are capable of making a completely fair and unbiased decision when it comes to weighing up whether they should play or not. The long-term dangers of playing while injured rarely come into the mind of most players. The real problem is always dominated by the next fixture – depending upon which team it is against.

Starting to play again before a broken bone has had the chance to reset properly or a torn ligament or pulled muscle has had the chance to become strong again is all too common in rugby. But the major danger is starting again too soon following a bump on the head – especially when concussion has occurred. Rugby captains and committees should take a far greater responsibility when it comes to deciding whether to select players who have received head knocks in the immediate past. The masochism should be ignored and players be firmly told, 'You are nor playing.' Most of the time this will not be appreciated at all, but much can now be made of Bill Beaumont's premature retirement from the pinnacle of British rugby. Bill was a man's man, a player's player, and no softy. If he in his position can turn his back on rugby in the name of self-preservation, his decision must be seen as a pointer to others, especially at lower levels, to follow suit. Bill Beaumont will probably never be able to fully appreciate the far-reaching effect his sensible decision will have, and should have, on the rugby players in this country or anywhere else in the world, for that matter, where the game is played.

The normal wear and tear of rugby is demanding enough on anyone's body, but because I have played too often with injuries yet unhealed, I dread to think what state I am going to be in by the time I reach the age of sixty. I know how many joints are currently bothering me at the 'tender' age of thirty-five, so my only hope is that some time during the next decade or so a remedy is found for arthritis.

Because of what I have inflicted on myself through stupidity and pigheadedness, I am a firm believer that rugby players generally – because I am not alone – can

cause more long-term damage to themselves by continually playing with injuries than any thug whom they will
encounter on the field of play will ever do to them. I may
still carry mental scars from my attack by Allan Hardie
but, thankfully, the physical scarring is now almost invisi-
ble. The scars which I have inflicted on myself throughout
my career will be with me till I die!

Having said all that, I also have to confess that my
playing with injuries was not confined to rugby. I broke a
bone in my hand in the third Test in South Africa in 1974
and that ended the playing part of the tour for me, but only
so far as the playing of rugby was concerned. One game
which I was still able to play was golf – against Gary
Player. Gareth Edwards and I had been due to play the
game before the second Test but Gary called off at the last
moment. We were disappointed because we honestly did
not think that the game would be played thereafter. Some
of the boys, Bobby Windsor especially, gave Gareth and
me a really hard time of it. Cheeky remarks abounded at
the training sessions. 'Big game today then?' 'Saving
yourselves for the golf this afternoon?' Bobby was the chief
leg-puller and he was beginning to bug both of us.

You can understand why I reacted to a phone call to my
room during the final week of the tour from a caller who
was purporting to be Gary Player when I told him to 'get
lost'. The caller was adamant that he was Gary Player,
but I was convinced that he was Bobby Windosr kidding
on. But it was Gary Player! He had only just returned to
South Africa after winning the British Open golf championship at Royal Lytham St Annes and he inquired if
there was any chance of a challenge match that week. I
excitedly arranged for Gareth, Mike Gibson and me to
play with him two days later at his old club Killarney in
Johannesburg where he started as a pro at fifteen years of
age.

When Gareth and Mike heard the news, they did not
believe me. The newspapers that night carried the story,
however, and that convinced them. I of course did not tell

Gary that my hand was in a plaster cast due to the broken bone. I did not want to scare him off. I had it removed on the morning of the match and when I met him I shook hands with my left hand. When I explained my predicament, he exclaimed, 'I'm sorry that you are not going to be able to play.' To which I replied, 'Oh, but I am.' The look on his face said, My God, what have I got myself into?

The match caused a real stir in the club. All the old members, some of whom had sponsored Gary on his first sortie abroad years ago, turned up to see their hero. Not only had he just won the Open, but this was his first visit to the club for a long time.

One of the members supplied me with a handful of pain-killing tablets to relieve my hand problem and we duly took to the first tee. Mike and I were to play against Gareth and Gary, and I was the first to drive. The crowd, a few hundred strong, formed a large V-shape away from me. I do not know what they were expecting, but the thought running through my head was not 'Am I going to kill somebody?' but 'How many am I going to kill?'

A large television camera, whirring loudly, was perched on a tripod barely four yards away from me – just off the line of play! As I addressed the ball, I looked at the shaft of my driver and it was shaking like mad. I looked at the ball and it was blurred. There was only one thing left for me to do – walk away. I had to, because there was no way I could have swung the club to hit the ball. With some jeers ringing in my ears I returned to the ball and very quickly hit it. It flew right up the middle of the fairway and I was delighted.

I must be the only guy in the world who has been brazen enough to take on Gary Player with a broken hand. Despite the pain-killing tablets, I was still in pain but I nevertheless enjoyed that round of golf immensely. I hope Gary Player did too. For the record we lost four and two. That night we were the guests of the Player family at their ranch in Johannesburg and we had a marvellous time listening to his humorous, and serious, stories. It was a wonderful ending to a wonderful tour.

11

In Stitches but not Laughing

A lifetime of happiness; – no man
alive could bear it; – it would
be hell on earth
— George Bernard Shaw

Rugby football is dangerous enough as a game without the
players being subjected to deliberate physical assaults,
but it would be idle to pretend that these do not occur far
more often than they should. I seem to have been on the
receiving end of a good few of them myself, and I have
sometimes wondered if that was just an unfortunate
coincidence, or whether it was because my brother Peter
and I never played the game that way ourselves, and
therefore we were regarded as a soft option, an easy target
who would not retaliate. Maybe it was simply because we
had been successful, and so other players wanted to have a
go at us just because we were who we were. I believe Errol
Flynn used to have just the same problem. Everyone in
Hollywood and elsewhere in America who had a good
right hand wanted to fight him!

Whatever the truth of the matter, neither of these
considerations could have applied to me when I first
became the victim of such an assault. I had just left Marr
and had had only half a dozen games for West of Scotland
and nobody had ever heard of me. I was playing for West
against Glasgow Academicals at Burnbrae. It was our
annual local derby, normally a game in which all that is
good about rugby is displayed. Midway through the first
half, I fielded a kick-off by Accies following our second
score of the match. A maul formed around me and in my

169

efforts to get the ball back to my scrum half, the maul collapsed in a heap. I had released the ball to a team mate just as this happened and found myself pinned on the ground, lying on my side with my head sticking out on the Academicals' side when an Accies player raked his boot right across my head – twice!

I yelled at the piercing pain but was unable to move at all because of the pile of bodies on top of me. The blood was spurting from the wound and I was panicking. I could hear yells of horror coming from the spectators, the incident having happened barely five yards from touch and right in front of the stand. As the players got up, one of the Accies looked at me and remarked, 'Jesus Christ! Who did that?' I eventually struggled to my feet and I was furious! I searched all the Accies' faces looking for the culprit to seek some form of retribution – but there was nothing doing. They all looked totally innocent. The referee had been blinded so he could not single out anybody. I was getting dizzy from loss of blood – it was still spurting past my eyes and my shirt was becoming sodden. As I was taken from the field to the club house, I was still raging and still in the dark as to who had been my assailant. The doctor duly arrived and after one quick look exclaimed, 'I'm not touching that! Get an ambulance immediately.' It transpired that my right ear was split in half. No ambulance could be summoned so eventually one of the West members, Joe Thompson, took me to hospital in his car. A turban of bandages round my head seemed to have stopped the bleeding.

I arrived at the hospital to discover a queue of injured sportsmen, all still in their gear like me. Peculiarly, most of them were soccer players. After what seemed like hours, during which I kept asking myself the question, 'Who? Who? Who?' I was finally attended to. By now the bandage had congealed on my ear and head. Removing it was unbelievably painful. Eventually a very young doctor stitched the two halves of my ear back together again and sent me back to the waiting room. I was later told by a nurse to go home and give a letter to my doctor. As I was leaving I bumped into the young doctor who had done the stitching and he was horrified to see that my ear had swollen like a balloon. 'You can't go home like that!' he exclaimed, and took me back in again! He removed some of the stitches in order to release the blood which had gathered inside the wound. He stitched me up again once he was sure the bleeding had stopped.

By this time I had been joined in the hospital by Quintin Dunlop, the West hooker and a fellow Ayrshire man, who chauffeured me all over the country and without whom journeying to and from West would have been virtually impossible. The constant question of 'Who?' which had been pounding in my head ever since the incident was answered by Quintin. 'Stuart Hardie, the Accies prop-forward. He was to blame.' I did not even know what he looked like.

With the referee not having seen the incident and therefore unable to authorize the SRU to take any action, it is to Glasgow Academical Rugby Club's great credit that they suspended Hardie themselves. Two years later, I was at Ayr Rugby Club's annual sevens tournament and West were sharing a changing room with Glasgow Accies. At one stage between ties, I went into the dressing room to change my boots and there was one Accies player doing the same. After a few silent moments I said to him, 'Is Stuart Hardie down with your team today?'

'Yes,' he replied.

'What does he look like?' I asked.

He paused and replied, 'I'm Stuart Hardie!'

Well, you could have knocked me down with a toothbrush. He looked normal, human, quite soft-spoken, no horns, no broken teeth, no drooling, dribbling mouth, no patch over his eye nor hook at the end of his arm! The thug in today's game is just an ordinary person. Quite frightening, isn't it? I just felt cold, and silently left the dressing room and changed my boots somewhere else.

Happily there were very few occasions when things

became too ugly at club level, but one occasion when matters did get right out of hand was in the most important fixture on West's calendar – the match against Hawick, at Mansfield Park, Hawick, in the old unofficial championship. An enormous crowd, numbering thousands, turned up for the battle of the giants and we dished up a contest full of exhilarating running rugby, powerful play and disgraceful, bitter punch-ups! The tension of the match increased the longer the game ran and with the score tied at 9 points all going into the last ten minutes, tempers boiled over completely.

I smother-tackled Jim Renwick as he came inside on a crash ball move and held him up off the ground with me between him and his team mates. A large maul quickly built up with the Hawick forwards trying desperately to get to Jim to help him retain possession. My presence was the main stumbling block to them and Norman Pender, the Hawick prop, decided to remove me. His method was to put his hands over the top of my head and with his fingers gouging my eyes, haul me backwards over the top of the maul. I did not approve of this one bit. So I released Renwick, twisted round and punched Pender as hard as I could.

In an instant I felt as though I was back in New Zealand again. The packs were belting one another with the referee an idle spectator. Eventually things settled down, but the final flurry was between Pender and Bob Haldane, the West wing forward; the referee promptly sent them off! Pender certainly deserved it as he had started it all and had also been involved in most of the niggle which had been prevalent throughout the game. The referee, Duncan Spink, planned to retire after the game and I am sure that if he had not announced the fact before the game, then he would have done so afterwards. He was certainly not on the same wavelength as the players and underestimated our physical and mental commitment. Consequently the game was never in his control and the final eruption was virtually inevitable. My commitment to the task of winning was such that as we entered the last five minutes of play, I was exhausted. I even went to the lengths of telling Quintin Dunlop, our skipper, to ignore me in the line-out from then on. I must have been tired to do that because normally I was after every line-out call.

Hawick won the match 12 points to 9, with Jim Renwick kicking the winning goal in the last few minutes. The final drama for me was being flayed on the back with an umbrella by a woman Hawick supporter while I was clapping the Hawick players off the pitch at full time. What would she have done to me if Hawick had lost?

The following week I was in Wales for the Barbarians Easter tour and I was picked to play against Cardiff. Before the match Bill McLaren (the Hawick stalwart and magnificent BBC commentator who has done as much for rugby with his presentation as has the Australian dispensation rule) came up to me with a twinkle in his eye and said, 'You'll no' be playin' it as hard for the Baa-Baas today as you were for the West last Saturday?'

I replied, slightly embarrassed, 'I hope it won't be necessary.'

How wrong I was. There was no championship at stake but the Cardiff forwards were getting stuck into us as if their lives depended on it. I was punched in the face in the first line-out by Ian Robinson, the Cardiff lock. I knew that I had to get my own back in the next line-out because I had heard that he was a bit of a bully-boy; if I was happy to take it, he would be happy to give it to me.

I hit him at the next line-out. It was nothing earth-shattering, more a 'get lost and leave me alone' gesture. But all hell broke loose. I was set upon by three or four of his fellow pack members and I can well remember in the middle of the swinging and dodging of punches searching over my shoulder for my own team mates' assistance. I was alone! When I eventually extricated myself, I made a very quick simple decision: 'I'm not going to die in Wales with a Baa-Baas jersey on my back.' Subsequently I played at a level of commitment which kept me out of harm's way. With the Cardiff pack rampant and Gareth Edwards and Barry John in devastating form at half back, Cardiff ran up 40 points. The Baa-Baas committee were quick to applaud the Cardiff display but at the same time could not hide their extreme disappointment at the result.

Very late that night after much commiserating over our cups, I was confronted by Micky Steele-Bodger, a Baa-Baas committee man, who duly expressed his disgust at my lack of 'commitment and drive'. He bawled at me, 'You were invited to play to your Lions level and we'll settle for nothing less!' The exchanges between the two of us became more heated by the second and he would not leave me in peace. My tolerance was fast evaporating! I finally appealed to Geoff Windsor-Lewis, the Baa-Baas secretary, to get him out of my sight before something really silly happened. Fortunately Geoff obliged and Steele-Bodger and I kept out of each other's way for the rest of the tour.

I thought that I was up against it physically again in the next match of the tour against Swansea. The lock forward opposing me that day belted me with his elbow in the first line-out and shouted, 'Oy!' at the same time. Before I could do anything, Merve the Swerve Davies grabbed me and said, 'Cool it, Stooks,' using an abbreviated version of one of my nicknames, Stoochie, from the 1971 Lions tour. 'He's got a nervous twitch – that's all!' *He* was Geoff Wheel and we both settled down thereafter to a very hard but fair contest which I enjoyed.

Incidents during international matches involving the Four Home Unions have been few and far between, but against Ireland in Dublin in 1974 I had my forehead split open after a wild boot clipped me in a ruck. The blood was spewing from the wound when Ken Kennedy, the Irish hooker and a doctor, came over to me. He quickly applied the correct pressure on the wound to stop the blood and said to me, 'You'll have to go off, Broonie, and get this stitched.'

Fearing some gamesmanship from this wily campaigner, I retorted 'Bugger off!' and knocked his hand away.

'Don't be such a stupid idiot,' he said indignantly. 'I'm saving you from bleeding to death.'

The Scottish team doctor agreed with Kennedy and I was immediately taken off to have the wound stitched. I was back on the field within two and a half minutes thanks to Donald McLeod!

Even playing seven-a-side rugby I was sometimes in the wars. I was playing for West against Hawick at the Gala sevens when I had my head split open during an accidental collision between myself and Watt Davies, who was the nearest thing to perpetual motion I have ever seen on a rugby field. As I was being led off my head was bleeding heavily but the enormous sponge that I was holding to the wound was soaking it all up. As I reached the touch-line in front of the stand, thinking in my dazed state that the sponge was full of water I squeezed it. The result was a cascade of blood all over me and an enormous gasp from the crowd, who thought that all of a sudden my head had burst open.

The vast majority of the serious incidents of thuggery have involved touring games. My introduction to the world of touring was when Scotland visited Argentina in 1969. I played in the first match of the tour and can remember thinking to myself after about fifteen minutes of general kicking and punching, if this is international rugby you can keep it! In the end we took firm control of the proceedings – which was more than the referee managed! – and won comfortably in the end. But we took the rough stuff as an indication of what lay ahead. We were not to be disappointed!

The first Test was a classic case of complete over-motivation. The Argentinians – the Pumas – had been living together at a training camp in the mountains for almost one month before the game. So much for amateurism and the International Rugby Board's rulings regarding restrictions on team gatherings before an international. The dressing room after the first Test, which we lost, was a disaster area. Never had I seen so many bloodied bodies, nor players weeping with shock. I walked out of the room, into the fresh air, nauseated and burning with anger. I asked myself, Is this what big-time rugby is really all about? During the next decade I was fortunately to find a happy answer.

The dangerous incidents in Argentina were not all confined to the rugby arena. One day a few of us were out walking down one of Buenos Aires's popular streets when suddenly a maniac produced a gun and started spraying bullets everywhere. We dived immediately for cover with our hearts pounding like mad. The gunman was over-powered eventually, not I hasten to add by us, and we resumed our stroll.

The Argentinians did not leave their fiery Latin temperament behind when they toured Scotland. I played against them twice: first for Glasgow and then for Scotland. The Glasgow game was a hard battle with several gey tousy and ugly scenes. One Argentinian, the prop Fariello, was constantly in the thick of things, not nice things!

The international match was a curious affair. We played abysmally and failed to score a try although we defeated them 12–11. They played well and scored two tries in the process. In fact, Colin Telfer's drop goal right at the end was a life-saver for us, but it was the last straw for them. They reacted violently to the score. There had been quite a few incidents during the game but between Telfer's goal and full time absolute uproar ensued. In the last minutes we went down into a scrum inside our own 25 and it was our put-in. As the heads of the front row came together, their tight-head prop Roberto Fariello deliberately kicked our hooker Duncan Madsen full in the face. The wound later required stitching. The front rows immediately erupted and I let the culprit have it right between the eyes, knocking him clear out of the scrum! The referee quickly stepped in to calm things and awarded us a penalty. We kicked the ball safely to touch around halfway and as we trotted down to form the line-out the referee blew his whistle for full time. I kept on running because I wanted to get to the tunnel before all the spectators started jumping and bumping into me as I had a sizeable hole at the base of my right calf muscle, having been stamped on by an Argentinian early in the game, and it was killing me. I had no sooner got to the mouth of the tunnel and started clapping in the Argentinians when I was belted in the head by something hard and heavy. It was a fist and it belonged to Fariello. The force of the punch knocked me down and dazed me momentarily. I remember thinking, I don't believe it. I've actually been punched after the game.

My father saw the incident at close quarters and, though normally a very easy-going fellow, he flew up the tunnel after the fast-escaping Fariello. The SRU steward who intercepted my father told me later that Dad had been blazing with anger. Pity he stopped him.

The incident tended to spare our blushes a wee bit. All the papers devoted so much space to it that we were never really hammered in the press as much as we deserved for our poor performance that day. The saddest thing about the punch was that it detracted from the superb effort of the Argentinians on the field. The police inquired afterwards whether I wanted to charge Fariello with assault. The answer was no!

Touring Australia was no picnic either. Scotland's tour there in 1970 received an early setback. The plane developed engine trouble after taking off from Amsterdam and we returned to London immediately with some very scared rugby players. We really should all have gone back home there and then! The tour was very hard and generally bad-tempered and we suffered many injuries, some quite cruel. The referees were terribly biased and the non-stop programme allowed us little time for relaxation, a necessary ingredient of any tour. I played in all six games and it took me a full month to recover physically once I returned home to Troon.

Touring South Africa with the Lions was a marvellous experience and, as I have said, it definitely holds the number one spot on my 'Favourite Places Toured' hit parade. However, it was not without its flashpoints. When we arrived in Port Elizabeth to take on Eastern Province we felt that the way they played would probably give us some indication as to how the Springboks national side would play. After all, the Eastern Province coach, Ian Kirkpatrick, was also the Springboks coach, and their captain, Hannes Marais, was the heir apparent to the national captaincy. The game did not augur well for the Test series! It was a filthy, bad-tempered affair with the referee completely out of his depth. Thank God, no one was seriously injured, such was the brutality of the exchanges. It could have been Canterbury, 1971, all over again if we had allowed it. The main difference this time was that they started it and we finished it with something to spare.

The first real mass punch-up of the tour took place in this game. The late tackling and general punching and booting which the Eastern Province team engaged in – with skipper Marais and his loose forwards in the van – right from the kick-off, eventually exploded us into retaliation when we realized that our physical preservation was in our own hands rather than those of the referee.

The Lions had a series of codewords and one of them, 'Ninety-nine', was designed for just such an emergency. Midway through the first half, at a scrum on our head, the 'ninety-nine' signal was given and we all erupted, in Wild West parlance, with six-shooters blazing. It was a disgraceful act which I am ashamed to have been part of, and what was worse, it came from the cream of British rugby. But given the same circumstances, I would react in exactly the same way. I have my family, my life and my future to consider before I think of the good of rugby! That is not an excuse. That is an explanation of the realities of survival.

Early in the second half I knocked a ball to Gareth Edwards from the tail of the line-out and fell to the ground with Bernard, the Eastern Province number 8, on top of me. As I tried to get up to follow the play, he grabbed me and butted me full in the face. I swear it was totally unprovoked. I went daft! Still dazed from the blow, I sought instant retribution. I grabbed his jersey at the throat and began smashing my fist into his face. I do not know how often I hit him, but John Reason of the *Daily Telegraph* wrote that if any photographer had run out of film for his camera, he would have had time to head for the front of the stand to his filmstock, reload his camera and still be able to capture the final punches for posterity!

The incident did not end there either. The Easter Province wing forward Van Eyck stamped on my face while all this was going on and he was spied doing so by Stewart McKinney, our Irish wing forward from Dungannon. The only trouble was that Stewart was about sixty yards away! That did not stop him. He set off towards the fracas to mete out his own form of justice. Unfortunately, by the time he arrived, the flurry was cooling down and the punching, booting and battering had ceased. He arrived like a demented elephant and smashed Van Eyck in the mouth, poleaxing him. Things took quite a while to settle down again after that, but once they did, we had no more trouble. Eastern Province had got the message.

Our game against Proteas made history because it was the first time a Lions team had played a coloured side. The 20,000 crowd was mainly coloured and their support for thier team was fanatical. The general standard of ability of the Proteas was low. To their credit, they all came on the field with a will to die for the cause – and many of them came very close to it! Played in intense heat, it was a bitter, ugly game, in which they showed very little respect for the general laws of rugby. I have never spent so much time fighting on a rugby field in my life. The referee was a joke. It was the first time a white referee had officiated over coloured players and he was bending over backwards to be as lenient as possible. He dished out penalties and warnings galore but he never looked like sending anyone off.

I remember jumping in a line-out, catching the ball with two hands and with my props blocking in on me perfectly, holding the ball safely until the correct moment to feed it to the scrum half, Ireland's Johnny Moloney. Imagine my feelings when I looked at Johnny to see two of the Proteas breakaway forwards standing right beside him! It was laughable – no, it was pathetic. The fixture was a waste of time and we felt we were being used.

The shame of the game is highlighted by two facts. First, Alan Old, our likeable stand-off half from Yorkshire was so badly injured by a tackle, which was so late that even an Argentinian would have been embarrassed by it, that he had to return home following an emergency operation on his damaged knee. Second, the referee, Mr Katzenellenbogen, declared to me and some of my team mates at a cocktail party two days later that he had been under strict orders from 'on high' that under no circumstances was he to send any coloured player from the field.

The injury to Alan Old not only prevented him playing again on tour, but also cost him any chance of playing in the first Test against the Springboks. Alan believes, and a lot of people share his conviction, that at the time he was injured he rather than Phil Bennett was favourite to play fly half for the Lions against South Africa.

Instead however, he spent the day in hospital, hearing the game on the radio and thinking of what might have been. The Lions did not forget him. We won the first Test by 12 points to 3 in conditions of rain and mud and wind which would have been all too familiar to Alan's native Yorkshire. When the match was over, someone said, 'Let's go and see Alan,' so instead of heading back to our hotel to start the victory celebration, we all climbed into the bus and told the driver to take us to the hospital. When we got there, we sneaked round the grounds under the cover of darkness until we were all standing outside Alan's window. We could see him but he had no idea that we were there. We started singing his favourite tour song, and he suddenly realized that he was not, after all, the loneliest guy in town. Then some of us climbed in through his window, while the rest went into the hospital in the more conventional fashion, and in no time we were all crammed into Alan's small room. We sang and sang and sang. There was hardly a dry eye among us. For me, at any rate, it was one of the most emotional experiences of my whole rugby career.

The problems of violence and being injured took on a new image during the Lions tour to South Africa. We were back again at Ellis Park, Johannesburg, to take on the Quaggas, the South African equivalent of our own Barbarians. I was to play, in my tenth appearance of the thirteen games so far. My boots were wearing out!

This was an incredibly exciting and controversial match. The Quaggas played out of their skins and we were really hardpushed to win by 20 points to 16. An early opportunist try by Andy Ripley gave us the start we were after, but from then until nearly half time it was all Quaggas. We were under constant pressure. They scored a try and a penalty goal and the crowd of 51,000 were buzzing at the thought of the floodgates opening up. (Remember, this was the same crowd who saw Transvaal almost lower our colours.) Just before half time we broke out of our half, and after a bout of mass handling, I scored a try near the corner – my sixth of the tour. The crowd was not happy with it, claiming that the final pass to me was forward. My try took the pressure off us a little but not for long. In a ding-dong second half the scores were poised at 16 points to 13 for us and we were hanging on like grim death. We eventually broke out of defence and another superb mass-handling bout ensued. The final pass to me by Tom David hit the deck, but without hesitating and with 51,000 voices screaming 'Knock on!' I scooped it up and charged the final twenty yards to the line, where I was

181

tackled and forced over onto my back as I hit the ground inside the in-goal area. For a second or two my tackler held my arms so tightly that I could not ground the ball to score, but just as the referee arrived I ripped them away and plonked the ball down on the ground. Try given! The crowd went bananas. Maybe I should say they went 'oranges', so many oranges rained down on me from the terraces from the irate home crowd. Even a shoe landed beside me! It was ages before the conversion attempt could be made – no one blamed Andy Irvine for missing that one. I further incensed the crowd by gorging myself on the oranges which they pelted at me. Mind you, they were delicious and I was very thirsty.

In no time the Quaggas scored a penalty to bring the scores to 20 points to 16. I felt that they were going to score again and give us our first defeat of the tour, and that is what the crowd thought too. However, we held out the remaining minutes and much to the horror and disgust of the crowd, the referee blew for time. Immediately, the crowd burst onto the pitch and their vibrations were not of the congratulatory nature! One of them ran up to the referee and, as I watched in disbelief, knocked him to the ground. I immediately went after the attacker as he ran off into the masses, who by now were completely covering the pitch. I caught up with him and booted him on the backside as hard as I could. He yelled and fell to the ground. I grabbed him and began marching him towards some policemen who were frantically trying to rescue the referee. The attacker, on seeing the police, attempted to escape from me. As I wrestled with him I screamed at the policemen to arrest him. The policemen had Alsatian dogs and, pointing in our direction, they released the animals. Imagine my horror when the blooming things came at me! I used the attacker as a shield from the dogs and my screams brought the policemen hurrying to my rescue. I have never been so terrified in all my life.

The man who had felled the referee was arrested and I was given a police escort off the pitch because some of the other spectators were baying for my blood, having witnessed me assaulting the referee's attacker without knowing the reason why. It was only when I got to the safety of the dressing room and started to calm down a bit that I realized that my right foot was very sore. I had jarred all the bones in my foot when I kicked the assailant. I couldn't play in the next two games because of it!

Such violence never deterred me from playing the game. I had learned from my soccer-playing days as a teenager with Troon Waverley that violence unfortunately can be part of sport, whether from players or spectators. 'You've just got to take the rough with the smooth,' I was once advised by Ronnie Richardson, the Waverley's top player. I am thankful that my experience in sport has been that the rough part is grossly inferior to the smooth.

My soccer days with Waverley were happy ones. Being a boy amongst men, it was almost an adventure. We played a good brand of football, winning more games than we lost. Some of the games were a bit tousy and two incidents in particular stick out like sore thumbs.

During a game in Largs two spectators came onto the pitch and started fighting with our burly winger Roy Thomson. The spectators had apparently been upset at some of Roy's robust tactics. The referee's threat to abandon the match was the only thing that stopped a riot developing.

The referee in a game at Crosshouse was in no state to issue a similar threat – he was unconscious! One of my team mates had poleaxed him. The culprit's identity remains a mystery to this day. Our centre forward Tom Bell was accused by some, but I suspected one of our defenders instead. An inquiry by the Ayrshire Amateur Football Association shone no new light on the incident and in the absence of anyone owning up, the club was inevitably banned forthwith. That decision precipitated my move to join Troon Juniors where one day I played in a cup tie against Irvine Meadow. They had a right winger called Hooky Walker . . .

12

Playing for Scotland

Many people felt that I played far better and far more consistently for the Lions than I ever did for Scotland. This is probably true. The main reason for this is the fact that I revelled in being a full-time rugby player as I was when on a Lions tour. I was able to dedicate myself completely to rugby, playing and training for the game. I was eating, sleeping, drinking rugby football with the best in British rugby. I loved it and I responded to it. I was able to get my body into a physical condition that I could never achieve at home no matter how often I trained.

At home I was never able to discipline myself to training every day; I was never able to build up the same constant impetus as I could when I was on tour. On tour I was constantly challenging for or being challenged for a position in the second row. The pressure on me to gain my position at club or country level was nowhere near as great as it was on tour.

When I was playing on a Lions tour and felt a bit jaded during a game there were always plenty of players who could do something to lift me. This was less likely to happen when playing for Scotland. I gave my all for Scotland. I never came off the field feeling that I had not given 100 per cent, but you can only give what is within you to give. Often, the comments that I never played as well for Scotland as I did on a Lions tour stung deeply. I would say, though, that generally I had to work much harder when I wore a blue jersey than I ever did when I was in a red one. Consequently I was unable to do as much

184

running about in the loose as I did with the Lions, especially in South Africa in 1974. I can nevertheless recall plenty of occasions when I had a high work rate and won a lot of ball for Scotland and films I have seen of matches I have played support my recollections.

I tended to jump at the front of the line-out for Scotland because usually my partners in the Scottish team were Peter Stagg and Alistair McHarg, both of whom jumped in the middle of the line-out. On Lions' tours, though, I always seemed to make my name jumping in the middle of the line-out. I greatly regret that I never went to the tail of the line-out more when I was on a Lions tour, especially the 1977 tour to New Zealand. I used to love going to the tail of the line-out, whether it was playing for my club or for Scotland. I always enjoyed my jousts with Mervyn Davies of Wales at the tail of the line-out, especially after my brother Peter had retired and was therefore no longer around to look after Mervyn. Despite the poor conditions in New Zealand, we certainly could have used a peel ball round the tail of the line-out much more than we did. Unfortunately other than Tony Neary the personnel that we had in the back row had no great prowess in jumping, and Tony only played in the last Test. I am sorry I did not exert myself to do more peels. However, because of my slow start during the tour in 1977 I always felt that I was never in a position to be pushy.

When playing for Scotland it never ceased to amaze me how so many of my team mates seemed to go into a shell when they played away from Murrayfield. Time and again, we played at Twickenham or Cardiff Arms Park or Paris or Dublin when really, on paper, we should have won quite convincingly, yet on the day we always seemed to let ourselves down by never producing anything like the brand of rugby we were capable of producing. Oh, how I hated that bus journey on a Sunday morning from the team hotel in Cardiff to the airport and yet two of my finest performances in a blue jersey, in my opinion, were away from home. Both were in Ireland in 1974 and 1976. To this day I will never know how we lost the game in 1974. Ian McGeechan could have scored three tries and yet he came home having scored none. It is amazing how prodigious efforts can be completely forgotten in the light of a defeat.

One of my biggest criticisms of the Scottish team was that we constantly practised moves at squad sessions on Sundays which were never considered during games. When the captaincy was in the hands of my brother Peter, it was not quite so bad because he was always prepared to attempt the moves we had practised, especially if they involved him! My so-called inferior performances for Scotland were certainly never because of a lack of inspiration either on my part or from the captain of the day. I loved playing at Murrayfield. It was a brilliant experience. Who could possibly have played there and not given everything for the cause?

During my time in the Scottish team, we had tremendous scrummaging success for many seasons but that success was only gained by much hard work and that in itself drained me. When we played against England either at Murrayfield or Twickenham, the scrummaging was hardest of all and we certainly then did not always come out on top. Amazingly against England, though, I always seemed to have that wee bit extra in reserve. I think we can put some of that down to pure history.

During a Lions tour I was always further motivated by playing alongside so many brilliant, talented players. As the games on the tours progressed I was inspired when these players produced their own individual brand of brilliance. This happened to a lesser extent when I was playing for Scotland. Constant injections of motivation and excitement never did any player any harm. In reality, I received far more of these injections during a game on a Lions tour than I did at home.

Since I retired, I have had far more complimentary things written about me and my performances for Scotland than I ever did while I was actually playing. I am tempted to say that the people of Scotland don't know a good thing when they see one. They only see the light when they have to live without it. Plenty of scribes have written about the coincidence of Scotland's dismal record of seventeen defeats on the trot following my retirement. Far be it for me to draw the same conclusions, but it nevertheless makes lovely reading. Of the thirty caps I won playing for Scotland, eight were against the auld enemy England. They included six victories and I am proud to say that I was right in the van in all of them.

In South Africa, my eight tries were ample evidence of the magnificent physical condition I achieved plus the mental attitude I had at the time towards the game. I was bitterly disappointed when the Scottish Rugby Union refused me permission to go back to South Africa in 1976 to play there for six weeks. Their reasoning was that I was going to receive a benefit in kind because my wife and child's expenses were being paid as well as my own. They also reckoned that with a busy season ahead of me I required as long a rest that summer as possible. The irony is of course that during that following season the Scottish Rugby Union suspended me for three months. When my suspension was finally over and I was available for selection for the Welsh game, I received a magnificent boost to my confidence when on the day before the international from which I had been omitted, I received a phone call from Gareth Edwards, the Welsh scrum half. He telephoned me from the team hotel in Edinburgh to my office in Glasgow and said, 'Broony, are you really not playing tomorrow?'

I said, 'Gareth, you're dead right. I'm definitely not playing'.

His reply was beautiful. 'Broony, my boy, we've all come to Scotland. We all know that you were available for selection and we just did not believe that you weren't playing. We reckoned that it was a Scottish trick and that you would be running out on to the park tomorrow as hale and hearty as ever, with your eyes popping out like

187

gobstoppers.' He rang off by saying, 'I'll go and tell the lads that you really are not playing. The Scottish Rugby Union must be off their bloody heads.'

I wanted to play for Scotland that day but they did not want me. That was the day when I stopped believing in fairy tales. The season following my Lions tour to New Zealand saw me playing no rugby at all because of injury. During that season I had a long talk with Jim Telfer, then the coach of Scotland B. He told me what he expected from me over the next three or four seasons. He told me that I had a lot to do for Scottish rugby and that Scottish rugby depended on me immensely. I agreed with every single word he said. Sadly, subsequent events overtook these demands and these desires. I would love to have won sixty caps for Scotland rather than thirty, but, at the same time, to win sixty caps would have meant that I had to forfeit my home life completely. In the end that was not for me.

As I say, I think I had a bit less than my due, but in that I was not alone. Few people have put more into the Scottish game with less recognition than Bill Dickinson, who was Scotland's first 'adviser to the captain'.

Coaching and coaches were almost dirty words in rugby vocabulary in the early part of my career. The main reason seemed to be the thought that coaching was introducing to our amateur game the threat of professionalism. Fortunately, largely due to Wales, coaching has been fully introduced now at all levels of the game and has proved that it brings not professionalism but greater dedication and commitment to training and playing.

For too long, club and team captains had the colossal onus of motivation and of organizing training and tactics, often at the expense of their own fitness and form. Some truly gifted players have paled considerably on the field of play under the burden of captaincy. A coach has the opportunity to see the team as a whole and to see the players as individual cogs of that unit in a more unbiased way than a captain, who is right in the heart of the action and whose judgement of a player may be tainted by some petty dislike. A coach–captain relationship which dovetails perfectly is the utopian situation.

Coaching must never stifle individual flair. If rugby is to survive and continue, flair must be given the chance to flourish. The game needs and thrives on the likes of Barry John, Andy Irvine, Mike Gibson, Gareth Edwards and Phil Bennett.

Bill Dickinson, Scotland's coach during our very successful run, from 1971 to 1976, of nine championship wins in succession at Murrayfield, was an ideal forwards coach. He welded our pack into one of the finest and most competitive units ever seen at Murrayfield. His lack of technique in coaching the backs was a pity because he certainly knew how to motivate them. He constantly encouraged them to use their flair to the utmost, which they did, but up-and-coming stars, like Andy Irvine, Jim Renwick, Ian McGeechan and Billy Steel, required moulding as a unit and it was disappointing that an experienced and respected player like Ken Scotland or Jock Turner was not seconded for this purpose.

During Bill's reign as coach our record at Murrayfield was outstanding: nine championship victories in a row, plus victories over Argentina, Tonga, Australia, a World XV (during the Scottish Rugby Union centenary year), and the England /Wales Select XV, when we teamed up with Ireland in the centenary match. The crowds flocked to see these matches and the spirit of the team was such that we never let our supporters go home feeling anything but sheer exhilaration. International days in Edinburgh took on a completely new meaning and tickets became almost impossible to obtain. A successful international team at home (plus the vastly improved television presentation) sold the game to the general public in Scotland in a manner which at one time seemed impossible.

Bill, to my knowledge, had no say in selection and therefore had to work with what he was given. I know that Carwyn James thinks that Bill did himself less than justice by not insisting on having some selectorial authority, and that he devalued the job of national coach, but I am not so sure. Bill probably knew that he would not have got the job on any other terms, and that if coaching was to be accepted as part of the preparation of the Scottish national squad, he had to swallow his pride and make a start where he could. The players were grateful to him for doing what he did.

To my mind, he managed this task well, and probably the greatest example of this was in 1972 when Scotland played France at Murrayfield.

The game heralded a new era in the art of scrummaging at international level. Our new hooker, Bobby Clark, was thought to be more of a good all-round forward than a gifted striker. Despite losing the tight-head count by five to one, Bobby's physical presence (he was much broader in build than the conventional hooker, such as Quintin Dunlop, Ken Kennedy or Rodney Balfour) had allowed us to put enormous pressure on our opponents' scrummage by eight-manning them instead of striking for the ball against the head. We not only began to intimidate the French but we succeeded in tiring them too. It was an entirely new experience for me, having played so long with Quintin Dunlop, whose appetite for strikes against the head was insatiable. Our scrummaging went physically from strength to strength over the next few games and the overall success we gained sounded the death knell for the out-and-out striker with the narrow hips. All top-class hookers nowadays are required to cover their own put-in, to be broad in the beam as well as the shoulders, to be able to throw in at line-outs, to maraud around the front of the line-out, to get around the paddock at speed and, lastly, to be no shrinking violet!

Bill Dickinson's concern over Bobby's lack of hooking prowess against France initiated my having to withdraw my head from between the loose-head prop and the hooker when it was our put-in at the scrum. This put me in a very awkward position in the scrum – as you can well imagine – and it took me many special squad sessions and practices to become accustomed to it, but it worked! It enabled my hooker to get much closer to the actual put-in. Roger Conderc, the correspondent of the French newspaper *L'Aurore*, reported that something new had been born that day at Murrayfield. Little did he know just what.

Bill was (and still is) one of the greatest enthusiasts about rugby that I have ever met. I found his enthusiasm infectious, his motivation stirring, his car driving terrifying! He earned a very special place in the hearts of all those tight forwards who played in the Scottish pack.

13

The Role of the Lock Forward

When the likes of Andy Irvine and Gareth Edwards talk about the 'donks' of the team, they are, of course, referring affectionately to the tight forwards. Locks do much of the donkeywork from the beginning of the game to the end, and every team is only as good as its donkeys, even if you have super-stars like Andy and Gareth in your team.

Gone are the days when lock forwards did nothing but graft in the scrum and line-out for the whole game. The game has changed so much since the introduction in the early seventies of the Australian dispensation restricted kicking law that it is now not a misdemeanour when a lock is seen running with the ball tucked snugly under an arm. One day, he may even aspire to carrying the ball in *both* hands! Such a sight once invited the demanding question, 'What the hell is he doing there?' Nowadays it is part and parcel of the game. In fact, the charging lock can now excite spectators and team mates alike to almost the same degree as the flying winger on his way to the corner.

Modern locks must be much fitter all round to meet the new demands of the position. The importance of strength for scrummaging and line-out play remains, but now mobility ranks alongside strength because, with the ball now remaining in play for far longer periods at a time, the lock is required to propel himself from set-piece to break-down and then, on the outcome of that part of the play, to be able to move on again in support of attack or defence.

The days of plodding about from scrum to line-out to scrum are dead and buried and I thank God for that!

The fitness-training schedule of any lock should now contain a sizeable chunk of running. Obviously stamina work is essential as the game lasts for eighty minutes, but interval running must be part of the schedule in order to cut down the recovery time following any burst of exertion during the game. You are no use to anyone if it takes five minutes to get over one charge at the opposition!

Many players feel that during the season two training nights at their club each week is sufficient time to devote to fitness training. Anyone resting on this assumption will never be able to further his cause. It was always my experience that most of the time on training nights was taken up with coaching and practising moves, and I am quite sure that most clubs work along similar lines. So locks must have the discipline to find time to train on their own in addition to attending normal training nights. Most locks, because of their height and weight compared with their team mates', have to train that wee bit extra anyway.

The successful scrummaging ability can give a team a magnificent basis to work from for the whole game. It is my belief that the scrummage is the most important part of the game. The art of scrummaging is surely the number one task for the lock forward. For this, there is no substitute for practice. There is no limit that can be set for the number of scrums attempted in practice – as long as the practice session is not the day before the match!

The binding of the locking partners is vital because the whole scrum pivots on this. The simplest way is to grasp the waistband of the shorts, though I always preferred to grasp tightly my fellow lock's jersey six inches or so underneath his armpit. Grasping a loose and flapping jersey which will just move about is useless. I remember during the British Lions Tour of South Africa in 1974, Willie John McBride once binding on to me so tightly that I had to ask him to release it slightly so that I could breathe!

193

The most effective way for the lock to bind on the prop is between his legs and to grip on the shirt and shorts at waist level. It is essential that all the weight and power from the lock is transferred through the prop by means of the shoulder–hip contact between the two and not, in any way, through this binding. Otherwise the lock will only succeed in pulling his prop down to the ground, which is probably what the opposition prop is trying to do anyway! So why help him?

I normally put both my feet well back, with my inside leg slightly farther back than the other. My legs would be well apart to afford a good clear channel for the ball. This channel would be closed totally if the call from the pack leader was for a hold-and-drive.

The left-hand lock has the choice of putting his head between the prop and the hooker, which is the most natural and popular position, or slipping it out entirely to enable the hooker to sit farther across his loose-head prop and therefore be even nearer the put-in than the opposition hooker. The latter position is one which can only be used after much practice, but it can be extremely successful in ensuring one's own ball. This being a family book, I will leave it to the imagination of the reader to determine where the lock's head actually ends up!

When the lock puts his head through between the prop and the hooker, whether on his own put-in or the opposition's, his whole body position and effectiveness will be enhanced if he lifts his head and looks at the top of his opposite lock's head which he will hope to see staring ineffectively into the ground, thus fostering a rounded-back position.

The line-out gives all locks the opportunity to display their own personal ability at ball-winning. I emphasize ball-winning, because that is the essence of line-out play. The ball can either be caught two-handed or deflected to a team mate. Locks should practise both, of course, but should generally use their favourite method. The two-handed catch is the scrum half's dream but sometimes the deflection, which has to be accurate or it is a liability, can be the best attacking ball for the backs to use as the opposition have less time to advance their defences.

For line-out play, it is vital that the throw-in is deadly accurate and that the flight of the ball is the way the lock wants it, whether it be low and fast or high and lobbed. All of this must be hammered out at practice sessions, but I am sure that at most clubs not enough time is spent on this type of practice.

If the lock prefers a low, fast ball it is essential that as he jumps he moves slightly across the line of the line-out in order to position his body, or shoulder at least, behind the ball as he catches it. For the high, lobbed ball I always preferred to delay my jump until the ball was virtually above my head, thereby ensuring that I was always catching or deflecting at full stretch. If I wanted to keep as far away as possible from my immediate opponent to minimize his interference with my jump, I always stood half a step out of the line-out. From this position my natural angle of jump would take me slightly across the line of the throw, giving me a good momentum for any contact which might occur with the opposing jumper.

I always had a personal signal with the player throwing the ball in, which would vary his throw to me. This variation is essential if the lock wants to be one step ahead of his opposite number. I always found it easy to play against a player who had no variation at all, because as soon as I twigged what his line-out code was from the scrum half or pack leader – which I always managed early in the game – I knew exactly how the ball was coming to him.

The golden rule of the line-out is that the locks dictate what type of throw they want and what type of protection they require. It is up to the others to see that they get it!

14

Scotland – The Braves

My rugby career was great. I was fortunate to play at a time when interest in the game was growing incredibly and it was becoming more open and free-flowing, particularly after the so-called Australian dispensation was adopted in the early seventies. The game thereafter became much more enjoyable: I could expect to have the ball in my hands quite regularly and something of the pure slog went out of the game. The line-out laws were altered drastically by making teams in opposition stand well apart to allow an interference-free jump as far as possible. This cut down dramatically the amount of skulduggery I was involved in.

During my career I have experienced guidance, protection, assistance, inspiration, fun, drama, pride and happiness, all given to me by the many friends with whom I have played. Let me share with you some of my favourites.

Arthur Dunsmuir and Tony McGuffie were the two Marr props who safeguarded and guided me through my first four years in rugby. Arthur was a grand captain, whose call to us when we were lagging behind was 'To rest is not to conquer'. Tony propped with a strength which belied his physique and tackled so perfectly it was copybook. He wanted to be involved in every move, was irrepressible and inspirational – and still is!

David Paton, our right winger, was our top try-scorer. He was heavily built for a winger but ran with speed and an eye for the opening. He also had the knack of scoring from interceptions more than anyone else I have seen.

Our scrum half was a stuffy footballer called John Sharp who took great delight in taking on the opposition back row. John later had the audacity to leave Marr and join our arch rivals Ayr, a move akin to a Glasgow Rangers player joining Glasgow Celtic. He was virtually ostracized by the people of Troon. To this day some have not forgiven him!

Of the many stars at West of Scotland, none made an impression on me more quickly than centre threequarter Ian Murchie. He was big, strong and fast and played quite brilliantly in my first XV debut match, in which I scored a try, against Kelvinside Academicals. He consistently produced great form for West and was responsible for our gifted international wingers David Shedden and Ronnie Hannah vying with each other for the 'top try-scorer of the season' crown in Scottish rugby.

Ian was never capped for Scotland. For that he can blame the time when, in Argentina with Scotland, he was deliberately smashed. 'Murch' was blazing a trail to glory, such was his form. The first Test was hardly under way when he received a double stiff-arm 'tackle' from both of the Pumas centres, Jurado and Travaglini, as he broke between them. His feet came right up over his head and his collarbone was broken, such was the force of the assault.

West's hooker, and my great friend, was Quintin Dunlop. He lived for winning, constructive rugby – and tight-head strikes! His hooking duels, in the days when hookers *were* hookers, against Frank Laidlaw of Melrose, Derek Deans of Hawick and Rodney Balfour of Glasgow High, were so intense they almost dominated the game. He once took ten strikes against the head from Bobby Clark, who had just replaced him in the Scottish team. Afterwards I overheard one of the Scottish selectors saying, 'No one could do that without cheating.' He was so wrong!

Quintin was a great captain and some of his team talks were quite fantastic. He was an excellent tactician on the field and to his eternal credit we always used the moves which we spent time practising during training nights. I wish that the same could be said for other captains I have played with during my career, especially at international level. He played in both of Scotland's victories over England in 1971 and did very well in each against the great John Pullin. The following season he was, astonishingly, left out of the Glasgow District team, losing his position to a player who could not lace his boots at hooking. This denied him the chance to defend his international position. It was one of the many ludicrous decisions perpetrated by the Glasgow selectors during my career.

Alec Wilson and Sandy Carmichael were the two props at West. Alec, at loose-head, was a rare competitor. I played behind him in the scrum for so many years that I was second only to his wife Catherine when it came to who had had most physical contact with him. Alec enjoyed his rugby, and I enjoyed playing behind him.

Sandy Carmichael was one of the greatest props in the world. He consistently played splendidly for West and his skills as a player were not confined to the cavern of the scrum. His tackling was excellent. This was fully display-ed in Scotland's amazing victory over France in Paris in 1969. Twice he tackled so thunderously that Frenchmen were dispossessed as they dived across the line to score. His party piece, however, was the peel round the tail of the line-out.

The classic peel of all time was during an encounter with West's arch rivals, Jordanhill. After a monumental battle, Jordanhill were in front going into the last few minutes. We had the throw-in at a line-out just outside our opponents' 25 and I nipped back to the tail to encourage our skipper, Quintin, to use a peel. Ronnie Hannah's throw to me was perfect and I knocked it down to Sandy as he came round the tail of the line-out like a train. He gathered the ball beautifully without any break in his stride and set off with his head down on a bulldozing run to the goalposts. He ran through John Roxburgh, the

College stand-off, and with four other opponents on his back he ploughed over the line for the winning score. I was running in Sandy's wake and I can tell you that the crowd behind the narrow in-goal area were beginning to scatter in case he kept on coming!

My first representative game for Glasgow was after I had recovered sufficiently from having my ear halved by Stuart Hardie (no relation to Allan Hardie). I had to be introduced to the Glasgow team because I knew so few of them. One of them was nick-named 'the Beast'. He was the prop, Ian McLauchlan, and he and I were just about to begin a long, happy and extremely successful partnership that would take us round the world four times. Ian was a great prop and despite the fact that he was so much smaller than I was, I had no difficulty at all in scrumming behind him. In fact it was surprisingly comfortable.

One of our very first trips abroad was to Toulouse in France to play for Glasgow against a Pyrénées selection. We won the game handsomely and the celebrations got into full swing. The wine flowed freely at the dinner and just before the main course was served I nipped out to the loo. There I met Ian and we started to chat about the game and our chances for selection in future matches. As can sometimes happen, our chat covered many aspects of rugby and although I was conscious of people coming and going I did not for one moment think that we had been blethering for all that long. However, when we returned to the dining room it was completely empty, cleared and in total darkness. We had missed our main course, sweet, coffee, liqueurs and all the speeches, all of which had, of course, had to be translated. Some chat!

Before the Argentinian tour I travelled to Glasgow twice weekly for training sessions, which were attended by Ian, Sandy Carmichael, Ian Murchie and Chris Rea, all of whom had been selected for the tour. Weight training under the watchful eye of PE-man McLauchlan was part of the programme. I started with the bar – on its own! My ratio of strength to body weight was so bad it was embarrassing, and was a constant source of merriment, especially to McLauchlan and Carmichael, for most of my playing days.

Ian and I both went on tour with Scotland to Australia the following year in 1970. It was a hard tour with many problems. The selection for the Test match at the end of the tour caused quite a stir in the team camp. Most felt that Gordon Connell and Colin Telfer should have been the halfbacks instead of Dunky Paterson and Ian Robertson. Peter Stagg was omitted initially, only to be recalled after my brother Peter was forced to call off owing to a scalp infection. (I was none too pleased with the medical services which Peter had received, which resulted in his head injury turning septic.) Ian McLauchlan was also ignored, which was quite amazing considering that both the Test props, Norman Suddon and Sandy Carmichael, were carrying injuries.

On the eve of the Test I had just finished dinner and had settled down in front of the television when Ian came over to me and said, 'Come on, Broon, we're going for a walk.' He had a face on him like thunder and that spelt danger. Going for a walk that night was the last thing on my list of priorities but I replied, 'Sure, Ian, great idea.' Boy, did we walk. I do not know how far we travelled but it was bedtime when we returned and throughout the journey Ian talked and I listened. He poured out his intense disappointment at his non-selection and said he intended quitting the game as soon as he got home. He meant it.

The Test match was a disaster. We made too many basic errors and Australia played well in winning by 23 points to 3. Just before half time, during one of the many nasty moments in the game, I received a kick on the head and had to leave the field to have stitches inserted in the wound. When I reached the dressing room, I found Ian sitting there. He was so sick at our performance, as well as being disappointed at not being selected, that he could not bear to watch the game.

He did not give the game up after all. Instead he went

200

on to win forty-three caps for Scotland, captaining them a record nineteen times. He also toured twice with the Lions, playing in eight Tests in all. Of those games, he won five, drew two and lost only one. Not a bad record for a wee fellow! He earned himself a new nickname and it was so apt: Mighty Mouse.

I attended a weekend squad session in Edinburgh some weeks before the tour to Argentina in 1969 and I will never forget walking among my heroes, actually ogling them. I just could not bring myself to believe that I was really going to train and play in the same team. I shared a room with Rodger Arneil. He talked for ages about players, games and incidents and I loved it! I was on cloud nine. After all, he was a British Lion and I had always admired him as a player. I could not wait to get back home to Troon to tell my friends about him.

Rodger was a terrible man for sleepwalking. He scared the living daylights out of many of his room mates with his antics. Once, while sharing with him, I awoke to find him sprinting on the spot beside his bed. He was shouting at the top of his voice, 'Go, go, go, go, go, go.' I eventually got him back into bed and settled for the rest of the night. He would never have believed me either if he had not been so stiff the next morning from his exertions!

My wife Linda and I attended Rodger's wedding in a tiny, beautiful village in Leicestershire. After the reception, once Rodger and his wife Judy had departed the scene, we adjourned to a local pub. Peter Stagg was the only other Scots player there, though there were six or seven England players. We had been there for some time when suddenly the landlord came rushing into the bar shouting, 'We've done it. We've done it. We've beaten the Springboks in South Africa!' He was of course referring to the England rugby team's now historic victory over South Africa in 1972. Staggy and I cheered and shook hands with the landlord. Then it dawned on us that our English fellow wedding guests were all very quiet. 'Bloody hell,' said one of them, 'A victory was not on my script for that tour.' They all shook their heads and sank their faces in their beer! Staggy scolded them: 'You bunch of selfish buggers.' He voiced my thoughts.

The Argentinian tour was the first time I teamed up with Peter Stagg and Alistair McHarg. Staggy was a mountain of a man standing 6 feet 10 inches tall. He was a prolific ball-winner in the line-outs, yet he was never fully utilized in that respect. Wingers never seemed to appreciate how high they could throw the ball to him. Too often the throws were low enough for the opposition to get at, which nullified the tremendous extra reach he had.

He received one hell of a fright one night in Argentina. He was returning to the hotel along with Rodger Arneil, Sandy Carmichael and myself and we were all in good spirits having just come from a cocktail reception. We passed a bank which had two magnificient entrance doors, fully decorated with brass fittings and ornate designs. There were two massive door handles and quite innocently Staggy took hold of them and gave the doors a good rattle. Imagine his feelings when the doors flew open and out walked a guard with a machine-gun. We ran!

During my time at Marr I played soccer for them in the summer against all the other Rugby clubs in Ayrshire. Although the games were competitive at times, it was great fun to see just who had the co-ordination for soccer and who had not. One of the best players was the backbone of Irvine Rugby Club; he took all the kicks, was in every move and scored all the goals. He was Alistair McHarg. Little did I realize then the tremendous partnership that lay ahead for me with this gifted man.

Alistair and I played in the same team for the first time in the fiasco against Rosario, in Argentina. I remember being very impressed at how little effect the physical intimidation from the Rosario players had on him. I displaced him from the Scottish team on returning from Argentina and he was out of things until two years later when we were picked to play against France in Paris. This match was the beginning of a partnership between Alistair and me that was to last for almost six years, during which I was to become one of his biggest fans.

He is one of the most talented players to wear a Scottish jersey. He ranks among the greatest line-out ball-winners of all time. His tendency to play out in the open frustrated me at times, but then that was Alistair McHarg. Many is the time he turned up seemingly from nowhere to save the day for Scotland. Probably his two greatest games for Scotland were in 1974 just before the Lions tour. The first, in which he was immense, was in Ireland and the second was at Murrayfield against France when he produced a virtuoso performance, scoring a try for good measure. He seemed that season to have booked his passage to South Africa with the British Lions, but that was one honour that eluded him.

Jock Turner of Gala was very powerful and fast. He seemed equally at home at stand-off or centre. His decision to retire when at his prime was a sad loss for Scottish rugby.

Sandy Hinshelwood was the kind of winger everyone likes. He would go hell-for-leather for the corner, given a quarter chance. He treated half chances as gifts! A prolific try-scorer for Scotland and the Lions, he was a very strong and forceful runner.

Billy Steel followed Sandy into the right-wing spot in the Scottish team. Billy was from Langholm and portrayed the 'little boy lost' image off the field. On it, he was most elusive and speedy and he scored some great tries for Scotland and the Lions.

During the 1974 Lions tour to South Africa he entertained the whole team at singsongs with a lovely Scots ballad with some stirring lyrics that none of us, myself included, were familiar with. We all eventually became quite proficient at the words and adopted it as our official team song, 'The Flower of Scotland'. When we sang it during BBC's 'Sports Review of 1974', the reaction in Scotland was incredible. It has now been adopted by many of the Scottish soccer supporters as their National

Anthem. The song writers, the Corries, have enjoyed a boost to their stage act and have now an even greater cult following.

Alistair Biggar, the London Scottish winger, and I made our debut for Scotland together against the Springboks in 1969. He was tall and elegant, and in full flight could produce a devastating swerve. He was a deceptive runner because of his long stride but, by jove, he could shift. He scored some glorious tries in New Zealand for the Lions in 1971, but he did not make the Test side because Gerald Davies, David Duckham and John Bevan were in such brilliant form.

Chris Rea had the most searing pace off the mark of any centre I have seen. A gap had only to appear and – whoosh! – he was through it. Two of his tries for Scotland in consecutive games had vastly different outcomes. The first was against Wales at Murrayfield in 1971. Chris picked up a loose ball inside the Welsh 25, after Rodger Arneil had brilliantly caught J. P. R. Williams in possession, and bulleted his way to the line. Peter's conversion would have meant Wales had to score twice with only a few minutes remaining. He missed. Wales scored again and won by 19 points to 18. The second try was at Twickenham. He terrifyingly juggled Peter's long pass and sprinted over the line to give Peter the conversion to win the game. This time Peter kicked an unforgettable goal.

Andy Irvine is one of the greatest players in the history of Scottish rugby. A very gifted footballer, he has excited and inspired me with his play more than any other player. His match-winning kicks and tries are legion. I shall never forget his 16 points, including two tries, in the last ten minutes against France at Murrayfield in 1980, to give Scotland a victory that, until he cut loose, seemed a million light years away; his enormous kick in the last second to give us victory against England in 1974 after the English forwards had dominated the whole of the second half; or his penalty for the Lions from halfway, in the first half of the third Test in South Africa when we were under great pressure.

Andy has made some mistakes which have cost Scotland scores – even games. But these pale into insignificance in the light of what he has done well. Many people feel that Andy's problem is that when he is fielding a high ball he is too busy thinking about how to beat the first man up. They are wrong – he already has the first man beaten and is busy thinking how he is going to beat the second!

Ian McGeechan was a bonnie player and equally at home with a soccer or a rugby ball. A shy, lovely man, he was too modest for his own good. A prolific dropper of goals, he scored one of the most skilled individual tries I have seen. It was against North Auckland in New Zealand for the Lions. He received the ball standing still just outside the North Auckland 25 with almost the whole North Auckland team between him and the try line. He ran straight into the heart of them and with electrifying side-steps sliced his way to the line. He has a great deal to offer as a coach of backs and I do hope he is utilized fully.

Jim Renwick has been the most consistent player in Scottish rugby for the last decade. He was unlucky to miss selection for the 1974 Lions tour to South Africa, but his omission from the 1977 Lions tour to New Zealand was disgraceful. He did make a Lions tour finally, to South Africa in 1980. His try in his debut game for Scotland in 1972 against France served notice of what class and ability this young man from Hawick possessed. Great company anywhere, anytime, this very likeable centre threequarter – or stand-off – is fast off his mark and has useful sustained pace.

David Shedden of West was a very elusive and speedy winger. A footballer, he had superb anticipation and, to me, a quite priceless asset – he could throw in really well at the line-outs.

Nairn MacEwan was a real character. We used to pull his leg that he was only selected for the team because of his patter and humour. He was perpetual motion on the field and seemed to be involved in everything. A great mauler, he won us a plentiful supply of the ball by continually ripping it out of mauls. He travelled thousands of miles between Inverness, his home town, and Gala. But in the end he made it all worthwhile and received twenty caps. He was unlucky not to be selected for the 1974 Lions tour to South Africa. What a tourist he would have made.

His first cap was against France in Paris in 1971. He was sharing a room with Rodger Arneil and decided to ask that seasoned campaigner for some inside information on the French players, as a form of relaxation.

'What's this guy Dauga like?' he asked Rodger.

'Huge. A man mountain,' was the reply.

'Can he jump?' Nairn persevered.

'Jump?' said Rodger. 'He could touch the clouds if he felt like it.'

'Is he fast?' asked Nairn.

'Fast? He's greased lightning,' said Rodger, 'and he's got hands like shovels too!'

At that Rodger turned over and went to sleep. Nairn tried to, but couldn't.

Nairn's last cap for Scotland was at Twickenham in 1975. He was only on the field a short time when he received a horrible jaw injury after a severe tackle by Tony Neary. His home-town club, Highland, no longer have a number seven jersey in the first XV, because they reckon no one will ever be able to do it justice after Nairn's efforts wearing it. A fitting tribute.

Gordon Connell was quite a character. 'Just knock it back anywhere on our side of the line-out and I'll do the rest.' He did, too! An eternal optimist, he was always full of fun on and off the field. He had an enormous spin pass and practised a move in Australia in which from tapped line-out ball he would spin the ball straight to one of the centres. It appealed to me tremendously but was vetoed by Ian Robertson, our stand-off, as being too risky. Gordon played exceptionally in Australia, but his crowning glory was at Bathurst against New South Wales Country

XV, when he completely outplayed John Hipwell, Australia's brilliant scrum half.

Alan Lawson also possessed a long spin pass and he used it to great effect for Scotland. He was never scared to look for a clean break and had a fair turn of speed. His greatest moment was perhaps one of his two tries against England in 1976 at Murrayfield. The move was started by Dave Shedden's burst out of deep defence and after the ball had passed through a few hands, it was Alan who injected the final sprint to the line. The roar from the Murrayfield crowd was deafening.

Douglas Morgan was less flamboyant than some of the scrum halves I have played in front of but he certainly was effective. His pass was short by international standard but it was fast and accurate, which made up for that. He was sometimes too keen to engage the opposing back row but that was encouraged by a high success rate. He was a great motivator, especially for me in New Zealand before the second Test in 1977. Just before the kick-off, he said to me, 'This is for Linda and Mardi – and nobody else!' emotive words indeed.

I felt bitterly disappointed for him after our Twickenham defeat in 1975. We were going for the Triple Crown and either of two late penalty kicks by him would have sealed it for us, even though we had played disappointingly as a team. It was not to be and the press tended to highlight these two kicks instead of examining the real issue of our overall form. Losing Nairn MacEwan so early did not help either.

Doug's moment of real glory for the Lions came in the last Test in New Zealand in 1977. Following a peel round the tail of the line-out, he burst for the line to score with a determination and will which seemed to convey his message of 'This is the *real* me when I'm fit and given half a chance.' He had been dogged by injuries for the whole tour and it was almost the last week before he shook them off.

Ian Robertson of Watsonians had great pace for a

stand-off, plus the skill and confidence to run at and beat his opposite number. He is one of the wittiest people I have ever known, although his team talks were never lacking in blunt home truths! He has called me Dummy ever since I unsuccessfully partnered him in a game of cards in Argentina in 1969. It was in Argentina that he nearly killed himself while demonstrating to us all his supposed prowess as a horse-handler. I will never forget his break at Murrayfield in 1970 against England which led to Alistair Biggar's score for Scotland.

David Leslie must be the most explosive wing forward I have ever played alongside in Scotland. He was dynamite. His physical commitment was so intense he received more than his share of injuries. One of the great tactical thinkers of the game, he has had the thrill of sprinting thirty yards to dive over the try line against England for Scotland at Murrayfield in 1976.

If I were asked to select my favourite team from all the players I have known in the Scotland side, I think I should settle on the following:

Andy Irvine
Sandy Hinshelwood
Ian McGeechan
Jim Renwick
Dave Shedden
Jock Turner
Doug Morgan
Ian McLauchlan
Quintin Dunlop
Sandy Carmichael
Alistair McHarg
Gordon Brown
Nairn MacEwan
Peter Brown
David Leslie

15

Future Tense

I am quite certain that the major threats to rugby in the future are going to come from professionalism and the problem of maintaining discipline on the field.

As far as professionalism is concerned, there are two separate points to be examined. One is cash, the other, perks. I will deal with cash first. The day that someone walks into a Rugby Union dressing room and announces, 'OK, lads, you're all on £100 a man to win today,' – the game is dead. As Rugby Union is a physical contact game, there are too many opportunities available to nobble star men in the opposition and I firmly believe cash incentives would encourage this. I have no wish to see the likes of Andy Irvine receiving the treatment which was disgracefully dished out by the Portuguese soccer players to the great Pele in the 1966 World Cup in England. No cash must therefore change hands in Rugby Union to influence the outcome of a game in any way.

Having said that, it must be acknowledged that the demands made on players' time and energy, and the very nature of the development of the game into a vast spectator sport, are putting an enormous burden on each player's life, particularly at the highest level. It is an increasing burden. More and more countries are touring Britain each season and inviting British teams to tour abroad in return. This is good for the game but it also means greater demands on certain players. These demands add up to far more than just playing in the matches themselves. The squad sessions which always precede them are far more time-consuming.

The increasing number of international matches puts each player more in the public eye, producing better-known faces, popular figures, stars with whom the public can identify. Virtually every player loves to be well-known, popular and recognized. Most players love to play at the highest level. Most players look upon squad sessions as the price they have to pay for these rewards. But squad sessions are essential to organize and prepare the team properly – as long as the work done at them is relevant and of quality. They must be attended by all the players in the team and most of the players on the fringe. As no player can be paid for devoting this time and effort to an amateur sport, I firmly believe that they should be able to receive openly, if they wish, some perks. Endorsement of sports goods and sportswear is one field in particular in which players should be allowed to participate. This, of course, would open the door to general advertising. All Unions have a responsibility to their players because it is the Unions who have dictated the way the game has been developed and marketed. They have been aided and abetted by the marvellous presentation of the game through television. The combination has produced today's rugby stars, from whom there is a constant demand for entertainment, success and availability, and whose privacy is definitely a thing of the past. If players were to be allowed to endorse or advertise goods, I fully appreciate that some players would be in greater demand than others even though they are members of the same team. This would increase elitism, but I am sure that this would not create trouble even though rugby is a team game. Quite the reverse. If we were all of equal ability and appeal the world would be a boring place. In any case, the whole exercise of finding and choosing the best fifteen rugby players in one country is, by definition, an exercise in elitism.

Now let me talk about the problems of maintaining discipline. Nothing will have a greater effect on the game of rugby in the future than lack of discipline on the field.

Discipline must be maintained at all costs. No one should ever be bigger than the game at any level. In fact, there has never been a greater onus on referees and players at international level to maintain discipline. I would like to think that the days of mass punch-ups and of indiscriminate use of the boot in rucks are gone for ever, but somehow I doubt it. The danger is always there.

The appointment of neutral referees for Test matches has helped, especially where British referees have been involved. We undoubtedly have the highest standard of refereeing in the world and the proof of this lies in the very few serious incidents there have been at international level in Britain during the last ten years.

The major black spot was, of course, the dreadful game at Twickenham between England and Wales in 1980. It's an ill wind, though, and one hopes that that unsavoury game cleared the air for ever. The press build-up before the game was big and too emotional, the players' build-up was too intense, and the pressures from the public of both nations was devastating. Thank God, no one was seriously injured in the general mayhem that masqueraded that day as rugby football, though I fear that was due to plain luck rather than to lack of malice aforethought.

I am afraid Australian and South African referees still leave a lot to be desired, and in Australia in particular the game can still be far too physical. It is almost as though it is a prerequisite of the game in order to attract spectators away from Rugby League and Australian Rules football. One of the main reasons Australian touring sides to Britain do so poorly is because our referees do not allow them to play the game that they normally play at home.

I applaud loudly the ruling which recently gave touch judges at international matches the authority to advise the referee concerning any skulduggery they see on the field of play. In the past too many incidents took place on the referee's blind side, but in full view of the spectators and the television cameras. This, to me, encouraged the play-

211

ers at lesser levels to copy such deeds and the game was being damaged at the grass roots.

The international match should be a perfect example of what is wanted as far as discipline is concerned. All that would remain thereafter would be for every club to weed out and expel from the game the members who regularly commit dirty acts on the field. These players are always known to their team mates, and what all players must appreciate is that if they accept the thug in their team, then they are condoning every foul he commits each Saturday.

Too many club presidents accept their nomination for social and egotistical reasons. Very few sit down and think to themselves, What can I do to improve the game of rugby football? They could begin by rooting out their own thugs.

Many of the up-and-coming rugby nations like Argentina, Tonga, Rumania and Italy have problems of temperament in the game; their natural make-up is more emotional and their background in some instances less privileged than ours. If we do not present a firm, solid example to them, the game will not grow as I hope and expect.

Proper development at an early age in life is crucial. Too much pressure on the seven- to twelve-year-olds from teachers and, especially, fathers on the touch line can act as a complete sickener to a child and drive him away from rugby. Too much organization and coaching at an early age can stifle flair for ever or kill any desire to learn at a later stage. Mini-rugby or full fifteen-a-side rugby for the youngster should harness the natural desire to run with a ball and to enjoy rugby's atmosphere to the fullest. That should not be stifled, no matter how great a *parent's* ambitions!

I am sad that I am unable, under the current International Board laws, to coach this wonderful game at any level now that I have joined the ranks of the professionals. I took payment (the first time in my rugby career I had accepted payment for anything) for some broadcasting and articles and advised the Scottish Rugby Union accordingly. In time, I received a letter of acknowledgement confirming that, as I had broken the International Board rules on amateurism, I would no longer be able to play, coach or administer the game at any level. I had gone into that situation with my eyes wide open but it nevertheless hit home when I saw the ruling in black and white!

I can fully understand not being permitted to write articles on games in which I have played or on games where I have coached one of the teams involved, but to ban me from any coaching means that I am unable to pass on the vast amount of experience I have gained at the highest level. I am even banned from playing in 'golden oldies' matches and charity matches too. All a great pity, surely?

Some of the greatest names over the last decade in Britain suffered the same fate: Barry John, Gareth Edwards, Mervyn Davies, David Duckham, Fran Cotton, Bill Beaumont, Gerald Davies, Ian McLauchlan and Phil Bennett. Surely the state of the game is not so healthy that these players, and there are more in the pipeline, can be banned for ever without rugby feeling the loss?

There has been much publicity and discussion regarding introducing a World Cup competition to rugby. I am totally opposed to it! Such a competition would open the door to professionalism (i.e. cash incentives, no matter how they were disguised) and we could say goodbye to the game of Rugby Union as we know it.

At what time of our already demanding season would it be accommodated? In Britain, September is the only month not completely taken over by official competition and that would be far too early in the season for our top players to be in peak condition. The Five Nations Championship is the backbone, focal point and climax of our season. It would be devalued by such a competition, as would our current rugby calendar. There could never be a time of the year which would suit all participating nations and this would detract from the competition. Wouldn't all nations have to be at their strongest to give such a competition true value?

It is different for soccer's World Cup. Everything and everybody can be organized to suit the finals because everyone involved is professional. Rugby Union players are amateurs and, this cannot be stressed strongly enough, it is imperative for the game's survival that they remain so!

16

Finale

Three weeks after our return home from the 1977 Lions tour of New Zealand, all the players were together again. The occasion was the Lions match against the Barbarians at Twickenham in celebration of the Queen's Jubilee. Yet for some time, during the tour of New Zealand, the Lions had no intention of playing in this game because our wives had not been included in the invitations. We felt unanimously that it was unfair to return home after being away for three and a half months to disappear yet again so soon after. 'Player power' came into existence for the first time in my experience. At first the Four Home Unions committee did not believe that we would boycott the event but Dod Burrell, our tour manager, soon put them straight. We meant exactly what we said. Our wives were then included!

It was a wonderful occasion, but the game itself was a sore anticlimax. It should have been a classic to be viewed over and over again, with thrills galore. Unfortunately it was not. The Baa-Baas team contained many of the stars who had not been available for the Lions tour (Gareth Edwards, J. P. R. Williams, Gerald Davies), plus many players who must just have missed selection for the tour. We all felt that not only had they a point to prove, so did we. We simply had to win the match to prove that despite losing the Test series, we still represented the best of Britain.

The selection of the French back row – Skrela, Bastiat and Rives – proved just how much the Barbarians committee wanted to win the match and the choice of Mike Knill at tight-head prop proved that the Baa-Baas committee forgot the basic reason for the scrummage in the game of rugby, namely 'to restart the game, after a breakdown in play, as quickly as possible'. Knill must be one of the most destructive, negative props I have ever played against and virtually all the ill-feeling within the packs that day stemmed from his mucking about, which either delayed or lengthened each scrummage.

I damaged my shoulder further in this game despite wearing protective padding and I should have come off the field a good fifteen minutes before the end. Such was my commitment, however, to our cause that I misguidedly chose to remain. That decision cost me the next three months' rugby! Little did I realize at the time that that match was to be my finale in the big time. Thank goodness we won.

When I resumed playing in January 1978 with my shoulder at long last feeling fine, I hurt my back very badly. It went into spasm at the base of my spine and the pain was excruciating. I then realized just how bad Roger Uttley must have felt when the same thing happened to him. I was about to leave my house, overloaded with golf equipment and advertising hoardings which I was going to set up at a golf meeting that the Bristol and West Building Society were sponsoring. As the searing pain knifed through me I sank to the floor and managed to crawl from the hall into the lounge. I gently lay down flat on the floor and was to remain there for the next eight days! I played no rugby during the whole of that season.

Just before the following season got under way I advised the Scottish Rugby Union by letter that I would not be available for selection for Scotland's game against the All Blacks at the end of November because the date coincided with the date my wife's doctor had given us for the arrival of the latest addition to the Brown family. It was a decision which I felt was fair to everyone. I was determined to be present at the birth of my new child as I had been when my daughter Mardi was born. I did not want to leave a decision about the match until nearer the time and get caught between two stools and I felt better once I had made my decision.

I played for my club until a month before the baby was due but then I stopped because of the increasing problems which my wife was experiencing with her pregnancy. Just before the birth I was coaxed by the club captain Bryan Gossman into playing for West of Scotland against Kilmarnock. The game was at Kilmarnock, only nine miles from Troon. I made arrangements to get Linda to the hospital, if necessary, in my absence, and left instructions that I should be contacted at Kilmarnock.

I thought that I had every angle well and truly covered so that, come hell or high water, I was not going to miss the birth. I had overlooked the possibility of being injured seriously enough to end up in hospital myself, and that is just what happened to me! It was bad enough that I should end up in hospital, but what really maddened and sickened me was that I was the victim of foul play. Admittedly, my mind initially was not on the game, but I doubt if under any circumstances anywhere I could have expected to receive in the first line-out such a belt from an opponent's elbow that it burst my eardrum. Yet that was what I got from Bill Cuthbertson. He was not so well known at the time, but since then he has gone on to play for Scotland.

I spent the next twenty minutes trying to escape from the screaming pain in my ear. Believe me, earache at that intensity is even worse than toothache. I was running faster, jumping higher and pushing harder than I had done for West all season. Then Cuthbertson thumped me across the forehead as I moved in support of my team-mate David Gray, who had just fielded a kick-off. I hit the deck like a stone. I thought my head was going to burst. I attempted to get up because I did not want Cuthbertson to know just how much he had hurt me. I could not move! I felt as though my body weighed two tons. I just could not

217

get up. Despite the pain and the anger which I felt, I was also embarrassed. No one had ever made me feel like this before, not even in Argentina, South Africa or New Zealand. And to think that Cuthbertson hailed from Troon!

I ended up in hospital badly concussed but nevertheless determined to get home as soon as the X-rays were taken. I refused to be admitted as a patient for overnight observation and signed a document relieving the hospital of all liability. As I waited for my father to collect me, Mr Masood Zhaidi, the casualty consultant and a good friend of mine and Linda's for some time, spoke to me most seriously of the possible dangers should I deteriorate without medical assistance close at hand. He convinced me and I climbed into bed.

The physical pain I went through that night between my splitting head and my screaming eardrum was nothing compared with the mental anguish I experienced not knowing whether or not my wife was giving birth in another hospital in another town that might as well have been a thousand miles away. It was a long, lonely night despite the regular attention which I received from the nursing staff.

I am delighted to say that a few days later I helped to deliver my son Rory into the world. Will he ever know just how anxious I was about missing that moment?

I became very worried when my head pains continued fiercely for weeks after my concussion at Kilmarnock. For almost two months I suffered them until eventually I was sent to Ballochmyle hospital in Ayrshire for a brain scan. It was a most peculiar feeling going into the scanner room. Of course I wanted them to find something – my brain! – to indicate what was causing the pain, but at the same time I did not want them to find anything.

I had to lie flat on my back and remain perfectly still while the large scanner dome was lowered to within an inch of my head. The scan took five minutes and I was beginning to nod off when it was finally raised. I waited for quite some time in an anteroom whilst the film was being developed and examined. Imagine my feelings when I heard laughter and chortling coming from the next room. The doctor appeared and, smiling, asked, 'Have people been pulling your leg about coming here?'

'You bet they have,' was my immediate reply.

'Well, guess what? There is nothing there at all! The pictures are a complete blank.'

Before I passed out, he quickly added, 'I'm afraid the machinery is at fault, we'll have to do it all again.'

This time the scan took ten minutes, and of course I fell asleep. When I awakened, I was told that I was the coolest customer they'd ever seen. Little did they know that I had been doing all the night feeds for the new baby during the last few weeks. I was apparently snoring so loudly that nurses were coming from rooms quite some distance away to inquire about the noise.

The final results of the scan were negative in that there was no serious damage, and in time the pains in my head died down and finally disappeared. And to think that Bill Cuthbertson had the nerve to tell me that he thought I had only been winded!

My wife's health problems escalated after Rory was born, culminating twelve months later in her having an operation for the removal of a disc from her spine. During the whole of that period I did not play rugby at all. I found this to be a fairly easy decision to make because I had discovered that there was a lot more to life than rugby football!

I was delighted, however, to receive an invitation to go to Bermuda again to take part in the annual Easter rugby tournament. It was a great trip and it was good to renew all the friendships I made there on my first visit in 1977 before the Lions tour to New Zealand. Although my team, Bermuda Irish, lost narrowly to the Rest of Bermuda, it was a high-scoring, exciting, open game. I did not know it at the time but I was never to pull on a rugby jersey again. This was my last match and I could not have wished for a more enjoyable and happy finale.

Linda suffered a severe setback to her recovery and with a young family at home, rugby began to feature lower and lower on my list of priorities. It never managed to climb back and eventually I decided to call it a day.

Many people in Scotland and at my club, West of Scotland, whose colours and name I had carried proudly round the world of rugby many times, felt that I had turned my back on rugby in Scotland because of my suspension trauma. Nothing could be further from the truth. I felt no bitterness towards rugby. What I had come to terms with – and I have my suspension to thank for it – was simply that rugby had grown out of all proportion to the place it should have occupied in my life. I suspect that happens to a lot of players without their really knowing it.

The last three or four years have not been all that easy, but in that time I have discovered who my real friends are. I am delighted to say that many of them are in rugby, especially in the Scottish Rugby Union! I am for ever indebted to the Scottish Rugby Union's surgeon, Donald McLeod, for his great care and attention in helping Linda. It is the measure of the man that in the darkest hours of Linda's illness it was to him that we turned.